LIVING ON LIFESAVERS

RAINIER GEORGE WEINER

authorHOUSE®

AuthorHouse™
1663 Liberty Drive
Bloomington, IN 47403
www.authorhouse.com
Phone: 1 (800) 839-8640

Published by AuthorHouse 12/08/2016

ISBN: 978-1-5246-0319-9 (sc)
ISBN: 978-1-5246-0318-2 (e)

Print information available on the last page.

Preface

THE AUTHOR WORKED FIVE YEARS for the Arthur Murray Dance Studios during his six year attendance at the San Jose State University in California where he finally graduated with a Bachelor of Science in Mechanical Engineering in 1964.

This book documents and describes in all its color the mechanics and vagaries of what bears the title of the "Dancing Era" in United States history.

Arthur Murray Studios' unquestionably led the charge and provided the most qualified access to formal dance instruction. They may have provided not only the most 'fun to watch' dance steps, but also the most 'simple to learn' steps. "Arthur Murray taught me dancing in a hurry," became a phrase we all heard bruited across the media throughout the fifties and sixties.

So, if you have a good imagination, let's put on our dance shoes, comb our hair, step out onto the dance floor and see if we can remember some of those steps we learned so long ago.

Contents

Introduction

"Dancing can be magical and transforming. It can breathe new life into a tired soul, make a spirit soar, unleash locked away creativity, unite generations and cultures, trigger long forgotten memories, and turn sadness into joy, if only during the dance."

So notes the *New England Journal of Medicine* article, "Getting Motivated: Let's Dance to Health." The treatise especially noted that dancing can keep the body healthy as we age. Particularly, it cited scientific evidence that people who dance just two times a week reduce their risk of developing dementia and diseases such as Alzheimer's; all this in addition to strengthening bones and toning the entire body. A library of scientific evidence attests to the physical and psychological benefits of dancing.

My wife and I met as teachers at Arthur Murrays' during the late '50s and early '60s. We have in recent years taken lessons and attended functions at Murray Studios since the turn of the 21st Century. We found the instruction effective, enjoyable and designed to our particular needs. We received proposals for new programs in a forthright and sincere manner: a truly professional operation. Other students reflected the same enthusiasm and satisfaction.

My experiences as an instructor in the '60s saw the same professional standards at the studios where I worked. Differences did exist, however, in the marketing methods of the '60s and that of today. These differences provide much of the satirical humor of this book. In all fairness to the dance-instruction profession, we should reconcile these differences with the existing social, economic and business landscape of that era.

Consumer advocacy had not yet formed into effective cohesive units. And phrases like "buyer protection" and "customer's rights" had not yet become part of the lexicon of the government's regulatory agencies. The morality of marketing pivoted about the adage "caveat emptor" or buyer beware. Legislation did not protect consumers from lifetime memberships or large irrevocable contracts. Nor did a consumer have three days to reconsider the purchase of a large item. And no one could revoke a contract if it had not been presented accurately; (just a few of many examples of absence of the current network of consumer protection laws).

Managers could listen to sales presentations over hidden recording devices and make secret suggestions to the closing salesman. Usually large, always bold men could converge as a group on a timid sales prospect and literally beat them verbally, psychologically and emotionally into submission—and an irrevocable sales contract. These effective, though customer-abusive marketing constructs, were common in business enterprises involving selling. They were neither illegal nor remediable. The courts of public opinion at the time focused more on issues such as a women's right to choose, birth control pill justification and race and sex-preference discrimination. Consumer advocacy would have to wait its turn.

The '60s and '70s are identified as the "Dancing Era" in American history. Arthur Murray unquestionably led this movement. Born in Austria-Hungary in 1895, Arthur and his mother migrated to America in 1897. He worked originally as a draftsman in New York City's East Side. At night he and his father taught dance to some of the itinerant New Yorkers. He studied under the then popular dance team of Vernon and Irene Castle. He soon worked for them.

In 1919 Arthur studied business administration at Georgia Tech. To pay his way he taught dancing at the Georgian Terrace Hotel—or to any fellow students who could not run faster than he could. He formed the first "radio dance" broadcast and popularized the song "Ramblin' Wreck from Georgia Tech."

Arthur Murray had a proclivity for foot patterns (probably engendered by his drafting experience). He started his first business selling dance steps by mail. He sold "footprints." Subscribers could place these patterns on the floor, step on each and learn a particular dance step. The business had limited success. His business genius, however, would not deny him unprecedented success in his personally-founded business for long. In 1938 he opened his first "franchised" dance studio in Minneapolis, Minnesota.

After World War 11, the popularity of Latin music propelled ballroom dancing into the next outer orbit of popularity. Murray capitalized on this new interest by incorporating it into all of his dance programs. His guiding ethos, however, always remained the same: that he could simplify the dance-learning process. "If you can walk, I can teach you to dance!" Slogans such as, "Arthur Murray taught me dancing in a hurry," became the organization's sound bite to success. By 1970 over 3,000 franchised Arthur Murray dance studios were owned and operated in the United States. Franchised studios are run and operated independently by individuals who, almost exclusively, started as dance instructors. By the time they have the qualifications to buy a studio they have experience in all phases of the operation.

Arthur Murray studios have prescheduled events to generate glamour and excitement. The spectacle of the ballroom, particularly in the competitive function, ensures this. Combinations of studios have annual demonstrative and competitive events: a "Dance-O-Rama," where students and staff compete at all levels of training;

a "Spotlight Party" where select teachers and students participate in special presentations; at least two "Medal Balls," where students dance their final exams to their Bronze, Silver or Gold medal programs; a "Superama," where all national studios compete; a "Summer Showcase" to celebrate the season; and other ad-hoc events to celebrate historical events. All of these functions take place at the best hotel ballrooms involving several hundreds or thousands of participants. Those not dancing at the moment become spectators. Certainly, the many competitive functions make dancing so dynamic to Arthur Murray students. They became transformed from everyday housewives or desk clerks to entertainers on the ballroom floor.

In my experience, approximately 50% of the dance teachers identified as being gay or lesbian—predominantly the most talented and lifetime (career) teachers. The dance-teaching profession operated in its own separate environment sequestered from the prevailing bitter sexual-identification turmoil: No one "came out of the closet;" no one made gossip-worthy discoveries; and no one received clandestine "propositions." We knew who they were; and they knew who we were. In the '60s, gay liberation movements had not yet formed. Spokesmen for the rights of gays or lesbians were not needed at the studios. The dividing lines between straight and gay paled in comparison to the need to cooperate in scratching out a precarious livelihood in the dance business. An invisible bond formed amongst all teachers that crumbled the segregating walls of prejudice. We were ahead of the curve in that respect.

I placed most dance teacher's ages between 20 to 30 years. Most had only a high school education. The older teachers often became technical trainers in some dance specialty. Some aspired to own studios. Many of the teachers had some form of childhood training such as tap, ballet, jazz, show business styling, acrobatics or gymnastics (the lucky ones). They always excelled as dancers. Gays and lesbians excelled regardless.

In our participation at dance studios later in the 21st Century, my wife and I marvel at the age mix of the students: elders predominate, particularly amongst the women. We consider that somewhat unfortunate for the reasons cited at the start of this introduction. Certainly younger people could dance and enjoy the benefits of a lifetime of dancing. But the benefits to elders also abound.

In the '60s—in my experience— women in the 50 to 80 age range comprised at least 60% of the student population. Demographics as well as lifestyle may have contributed to this: Widows of World War 11 veterans and the male-dominated smoking habits of the '30s, '40s and '50s left many non-working middle-aged women without husbands; or husbands too masculine-minded to enjoy dancing; and women left well off with single lives and large divorce settlements. For all these women the studio provided a cloistered ecosphere of healthful exercise, mind-preserving learning and social contacts. And, all of the teachers knew their names.

The current mix of men to women students appears about equal. In my experience in the '60s, women comprised about 70 percent of the students. This created a male/female unbalance at parties. It also taxed the male-dominated teaching staff. They had to circulate efficiently to make up the difference. "I don't want to see women students standing in the corners," studio owners would say: a definite numbers problem.

The 1950s marked the "boxing" era. It started out with Monday night boxing. But soon you could turn on your TV on most any night of the week and you could find Monday Night, Tuesday Night, Wednesday Night or Friday Night Boxing. It literally overexposed the sport into obsolescence. Likewise the '60s and '70s became the ballroom dancing era, but with far less overexposure. Most large cities had at least one ballroom with a live orchestra where singles could meet and where couples could strut the steps they learned together. In the San Francisco Bay Area, we had the Avalon Ballroom across the bay in Oakland. Here, a live orchestra sat at the end of the spacious floor. Between dances one could sit in the upper floor circular balcony seats, view the dancers and converse while taking a break. Singles might sit waiting for invitations to dance.

Small "night clubs" sprang up in vacated soda-fountain, candy-store buildings. Each had a comfortable dance floor, Bars much the same. If you could impress the ladies with your dancing, it could make up for considerable missing elsewhere.

The contemporary television spectacle "Dancing with the Stars" has done much to revitalize ballroom dancing in the world. Teachers I know at one studio in San Jose, California attest to this. "Every time they have another series and a new line of stars compete the student enrolment goes up by 30 percent. By the end of the series -- the last week -- the enrollment doubles." I have noticed many new studios in the area. Hopefully the continued success of the show will usher in another age of ballroom dancing in both the United States and the rest of the world.

I hope this book helps to do this also. Don't get caught up in the particulars. Keep an open mind; and remember, "It was a different era."

Chapter 1

TRAINING CLASS

WALKING DOWN FIRST STREET AT the corner of San Carlos Avenue, Dixieland music blared out of a small bar. Just inside the doorway girls in light flowing skirts glided across the floor flashing white thighs at each whip-like turn performing what dancers call "West Coast Swing." The men strutted as they led with firm, unmistakable arm and body movements. As the anchor of each turn, they posed as a peacock would display its feathers for its mate. Others sat at the bar, or at the side of the long rectangular room, clapping with the music. They looked on, their eyes squinting in the dim light.

Drifting tentatively through the doorway, I nonchalantly scanned the room. Men sat mostly at the bar. Small circular tables lined the periphery of the dance floor. Typically, two or three girls sat at each table holding a drink in one hand and a cigarette in the other. Each had the same bored but observant expression. I made eye contact with one. I must have stared. Did she smile? The keys in my pocket jingled and my mouth felt dry. The bartender glared at me imploringly. "Can I help you, pal?" I glanced back at the girl. I hesitated for a moment taking a deep breath. Looking inside my wallet, a ten-dollar bill sat on top of a pile of smaller bills. Facing the bartender, I started to speak. Instead, I turned. My leather heals clicked on the wooded floor. Shortly I slammed through the double door into the bright sunlight.

This same scenario would repeat itself at night clubs and small dance clubs popular at that time. Or, I would take a friend, watch and

1

clap. During slow, well-populated dance floor numbers, we would sneak onto the floor and lose ourselves in the darkness and the crowd. Or we would stand, sway a bit sideways, take a step forward, then back and then sway again sideways.

I decided to heed the admonitions of ubiquitous radio, television and print ads to "'Let Arthur Murray's 'magic step' make learning dancing simple for you.'" It sounded good to me: a few hours, a few lessons and I become the young version of Fred Astaire. I signed up for an "introductory" three-lesson program at the Sutter Street Studio in San Francisco.

True to the claims of the ad, I learned the "Magic Step" in one lesson (I believe you could teach it to an Orangutan in two). It consisted simply of two walking steps forward and one side step—1, 2, 3 and 4 -- perfect three-quarter time rhythm, which fit most of the popular music at the time. One could repeat the step over and over again and keep in perfect synchronism with the music.

My teacher could not have weighed more than ninety pounds, but had each ounce perfectly placed. Her pitch-black hair, recklessly covering one eye, accented glistening white teeth that never stopped smiling, even when she talked. Miss Hertz—as the receptionist introduced her to me—could charm a concrete wall, and she knew it.

The remainder of the lesson time, above and beyond that required to learn steps—about 90% of the time—Miss Hertz "Juniored" me (The term Arthur Murray organizations used for processing an entry student with the primal goal of selling him/her a continuing dance program). Good "Juniors" do not overlook student self indulgence as a valuable tool in this process: she asked the questions and I regurgitated the neighborhood I grew up in, my high-school sweetheart, my interests, my opinions, my values and my greatest achievements. By the end of the second lesson she knew more about me than my mother did. Any remaining scraps of time she spent flitting around the floor performing advanced "demonstration" steps appearing provocative, graceful, and most of all, in perfect control. As per script, by the end of the third lesson I had become hopelessly infatuated with my teacher (had I chosen to continue with more lessons—though I did not know it at the time —I would have been assigned another "regular" teacher.)

At the end of the final lesson we sat down together and talked about taking what she referred to as "serious" dancing instruction. This term, "serious" struck me as odd. I would have classed my psychological state regarding what we had learned so far as bordering on frenzy. At the onset of the discussion I told Miss Hertz that I had limited resources: "I live on a cache of money I had squirreled away in a savings account from my last days in the service. I will start classes at San Jose State University next month," I told her. "It has to last until I find a job. I don't have a penny to spare."

This did not faze her in the slightest. We sat in a small office adjacent a large ballroom. At times the phone would ring. She would listen, say very little if anything and hang up. The office sat sequestered from the swarm of moving bodies and music outside the doorway. She would often place one hand over her ear. At one time a young man with a thin mustache wearing a red jacket, bow tie and flashing a wide smile entered the room unannounced. He introduced himself as Mr. Cleveland. He progressed through the same set of self-indulgence-provoking questions as Miss Hertz had previously. He finally asked what I thought of the job Miss Hertz had done in teaching me. I replied that she had done a fine job. I added, however, that she had attempted to abuse me sexually, but that I had been able to handle the situation. Mr. Cleveland's eyes blinked and looked startled for an instant. He then flashed his white teethed smile, chuckled clumsily and answered, "I'm glad to hear that you could handle it."

When it finally became apparent that no matter how hard they could squeeze, blood would not flow, Mr. Cleveland stood up, followed by Miss Hertz. As informally fast as our meeting had started, it ended as quickly: Miss Hertz merely said, "If you change your mind we'll always be here." She extended her arms, gave me a final hug placing her cheek softly against mine. I recall thinking, "If I sell my car, write another letter to my mother, pawn the ring dad gave me for my birthday. . . ."

Several weeks later, just as classes had begun at San Jose State, I moved into a "residence" club in San Jose. I met a young woman named Joan Darin. We dated for about six months. Coincidentally, Joan had been a teacher for Arthur Murray for a short time. She gave up the job to become a secretary at a law firm. Joan offered to teach me to dance.

Unfortunately for me—just one week after Joan had made the offer—a young man named Paul moved into the residence club. Paul looked like Brad Pit and talked like Clint Eastwood. He took an immediate attraction to Joan. I was asked to take my radio and record player out of her room. Before breaking my heart for the fourth time in my short lifetime, Joan taught me two things: first, the opening "break" step in the Cha-Cha; and secondly that Author Murray holds "training classes" periodically for potential teachers.

"But Joan," I said, "I can't dance a step. Why would they pick me as one to train?"

"Trust me," She responded somewhat irritably. She slashed at her long, pitch-black hair with a brush preparing for a date with Paul. "They actually prefer you don't know much dancing. You have less to unlearn. It's easier to teach you the right way—their way."

Joan's comments about the training classes festered in my mind for several months after our relationship ended. I moved to a new address where I did not have to see her holding hands with Paul coming down to the dining area for breakfast or supper. One afternoon, I took a deep breath and called the San Jose Arthur Murray Studio. They would start a new training class in just three weeks.

I bought a new suit at Rose Atkins, polished my shoes and had my hair cut one week before a phone message noted the studio would accept applications. That Monday I walked slowly up the long stairs of the old residential building converted into a dance studio on The Alameda, the main street of downtown San Jose. From the outside it always reminded me of the cryptic house looming mysteriously on the hill behind the Bates Motel in the Movie, *Psycho*. It had three operational floor levels. Exterior steps, winding up from the street, entered on the mid-level where the reception desk sat. Inside the doorway, that level had the bathrooms, the women's lounge and the several offices, including a large office for the owner. Separate stairs led down to a small, basement-like ballroom in front of the building and a large ballroom in the back. Each had floor-to-ceiling mirrors on opposite walls. The large ballroom in back windowed out into a small atrium—all very attractive decor. The top floor comprised five large "practice" rooms. Here, students received their private lessons.

I combed my hair on the way up the long steps to the entrance. I anticipated an interview with the owner and several of the staff. I tried to anticipate questions they might ask. I still fumbled for answers in my mind as I pushed the door open. A middle-aged woman wearing the name tag "Carol" sat behind the reception desk. Carol Dixon had a round face and body, and a continuous smile. "May I help you," she asked casually.

When I told her that I would like to apply for consideration to enter the training class, she perfunctorily said "Oh yes." She pulled a tablet out from under the counter and handed it to me. "Sign your name, and write down your age, gender and social security number."

When I handed it back, she took no notice of me or what I had written. "Be here next Monday afternoon no later than 1 PM."

At 1 PM at least 20 applicants stood milling around the lobby on the intermediate level. At about 1:15 a young lady led us all up the stairs to one of the large practice rooms. Here, we milled for another fifteen minutes. One of the candidates left the room and did not return.

Finally, a tall man of about 40 years of age wearing a name tag reading "Mr Fox" walked in and introduced himself. Bob managed the training class and also taught some of the steps to the trainees. Bob looked the part of the early twentieth century movie idol: tall and lean with dark wavy hair, fine, square features—a woman's dream. Unfortunately for women, even the young and relatively naive trainees recognized clearly by his speech and mannerisms that women were not part of Bob's dreams. And, though polite and hospitable, he had a disdainful, condescending smile that could intimidate the most confident.

Mr. Fox noted some of the "ground rules": working hours would extend from 1 to 10 PM; the training class would last approximately 15 to 17 weeks; trainees would receive no pay during this training period; they would learn the school figures (men's and women's parts) of all 10 steps of the "bronze" level of dancing in 8 dances—tango, fox trot, waltz, rumba, samba, swing, mambo and meringue; they would also have to demonstrate the ability to lead these steps; when referring to other teachers— as well as yourself—they would use only last names; and finally that the students would take three major tests to demonstrate these learned abilities. Mr. Fox noted that his standards for graduation far exceeded those of any other studio in the Arthur Murray system. "If that bothers you, now is the time to leave," he said curtly.

In addition to dance training, prospects received certain educational instructions in psychology—particularly in regards to selling, and proper dress recommendations. Most surprising to me, we received etiquette instructions on what constitutes socially acceptable manners. This included such items as what utensils to use first at the dinner table—a pseudo-dialectic charm school. Teachers attended many social activities with the students.

By the end of the third week of the training class the original number of twenty had dwindled to fifteen. The culling process came about not so much because of lack of talent or other positive attributes on the part of the trainees, but rather because of their frustration with the process. "I'll never learn all these silly-ass steps." Or "If Mrs. Fox corrects my missteps and looks at me like I'm some kind of idiot, I just may tell him to take his training class and shove it." Or, of course, "I can't live on dance steps forever. I'm getting awfully hungry."

I befriended a tall young man with prematurely balding hair and a wide toothy smile named Bill (Mr. Roper to the studio). Without Bill I surely would not have made it through the class. Both Bill and I seemed to learn slowly, particularly remembering complicated dance steps. Fortunately, what I forgot he remembered, and vice versa. Also, we could commiserate when Mr. Fox would rag on us over some step we had abused—not an infrequent occurrence. "Hey, don't worry about it," he'd say. "He's just picking on you because you don't look at him like some do—like Ford or Murphy."

As with all other aspects of life, trainees did not compete on a level playing field: those who had serious dance training in their youth—ballet, tap, jazz, or even those who did gymnastics had the greatest advantage. The gay men, for whatever reason, seemed to instinctively learn and demonstrate everything with style more quickly than others. Finally, the most disadvantaged group comprised those who were (or thought they were) good dancers when they started the class. As Joan had noted, converting them to a different style was difficult.

By the sixth week of the training class the field had dropped to nine. Mr. Fox seemed surprised to see Bill and I remain. "My mind is dizzy with steps," Bill said one afternoon as we sat in the Pizza Parlor across the street from the studio. "I see them in my sleep at night; I see them on the walls at breakfast; I see them when I drive the freeway: all the ten steps in each dance; especially those flaky meringue steps." He took time out to down a large bite of pizza before noting that "In class I keep doing the right step for the wrong dance. I notice you did the same thing yesterday using a Fox Trot step in the Rumba." He seemed ready to quit.

He seemed overly serious for a moment, reached across the table and put his hand on my arm. "Maybe we just aren't meant for this," he said.

"I know what you mean, Bill. What bothers me most is that I feel so clumsy doing everything. Like some kind of three-legged chicken."

"Especially after Fox glides through them like Fred Astaire." Bill said.

"Or ex-ballerina Hudson flies through them like on a cloud with Grace Kelley," I offered.

"More to the gut of things, the money I have in savings is going to run out in not too long," Bill noted.

I offered to loan Bill some money until we finished class but he refused. "Don't worry about it," he said. "I can always get a few bucks from my parents if I have to."

"So! What do we do?" I asked. "Do we give Fox the satisfaction of quitting?"

Bill did not answer. Instead he just ate another bite of his pizza. Later we both smiled and shook our heads slowly.

After ten weeks of class we had our first formal test comprising the school figures in all eight dances.

"This must be how they cull the chaff from the wheat," Bill noted, when he read the notice of the exam on the trainees bulletin board Friday morning. Mr. Fox seemed to look expressly at Bill and I as he announced that no teacher would make it through the program without a passing grade on all the steps.

"By Monday we have to learn all the steps. Some, I'm not even sure of the name," Bill commented that evening at the pizza parlor.

That Friday night we asked Carol if we could borrow the key for the studio over the week end. She glanced at Bill and I and spread her lips in a way as to register a coy surprise. When she handed me the key she reminded me to shut off all the lights at night. "We're not going to stay that late," I assured her, smiling.

San Jose has "Indian" summer weather in September and October. We found a cool room on the north side of the building with mirrors on three walls. Here, we sequestered ourselves for eight to ten hours each day and practiced each of the steps in all dances at least five times. One would call the step out from the list and the other would walk through the step—both men's and women's parts.

On Saturday night we did have to turn the lights off. Bill and I took off our shoes and nursed our swollen feet as we ate dinner at the parlor across the street. "I go over and over these steps, reading them from the sheet, but I still don't remember them the next time around," Bill noted. "It's like I never saw the step before."

With all the extra time spent on practicing steps, my studies at school suffered. Fortunately, I had only registered for twelve units of classes instead of the usual fifteen. I dropped three more after the fifth week of school. I could handle the remaining nine units.

When Bill and I reported for work on Monday, we received the best news of our short dancing careers: Mr. Fox received notice of his selection to compete in a dance competition in southern California. He would leave immediately to practice with his partner. He postponed the test exactly one week. This gave us an additional week to practice our steps. Mr. Fox had Jim Peters, an independent consultant, introduce "junioring" techniques to the class, originally scheduled for the following week..

That weekend Bill and I borrowed the key from Carol again and came in early Saturday and Sunday mornings. We ate both lunch and supper across the street. Bill and I still had enormous difficulty remembering steps. "I still feel like I'm rolling on stones when I move," I told Bill. "Do you know what I mean?"

"Exactly," Bill replied. "It's like I have one leg shorter than the other. Nothing feels comfortable."

When Fox came back the following Monday, his mood had an up-beat tilt. He had placed second in the overall competition for all the studios in the country—not a minor accomplishment. He spent the entire day testing. He would call out the step in a particular dance. The student would walk through the men's and then the women's part. He called out every one of the ten steps in all eight dances. The process took over two hours per trainee. Testing continued on Tuesday. The rest of the training class stood against the walls of the large practice room and watched. This put even more pressure on the performer. It also gave them the opportunity to see each step one more time.

Mr. Fox had Bill and I do our testing first—and in that order. I could see the muscles on Bill's round jaw ripple when asked to perform first. As he walked through the steps, however, his mood seemed to change: as he slid across the floor with his arms in the dance position he maintained a smiling expression—Fox's first commandment. He actually took on a look of confidence, though he certainly did not look graceful. And he did make several obvious mistakes. Two patterns he could not remember at all. After his last sequence of steps, Fox had nothing to say. He merely asked me to step forward.

My performance, more or less, mirrored Bill's. At the end, Mr. Fox, again, said nothing. He just asked the next trainee to step forward.

When testing ended late Tuesday, as before, Fox gave no indication of his judgments. Nor did we ever receive any indication of our relative grading. Obviously, some did better than others. Hudson, the ex-ballerina, never as much as strained on a step and looked as if she had been doing them all her life. Others did precipitously worse. Fox, however, as usual, said nothing. He merely asked the next trainee to take the floor.

The following week, Fox, in like manner, made no mention of the results or consequences of the testing. Miss Gambol, however, a young heavy set girl student with a turned up nose and pig tails, did not appear for training class the following day after the testing. Nor did Mr. Hall, a blond youth with freckles. We all just continued on. Miss Gambol and Mr. Hall did not.

At the end of the thirteenth week, Fox addressed the group shortly before 10 PM on Friday: "I think that we have all reached our maximum potential." He paused for a bit and looked about at the remaining seven candidates standing together. "What you don't know now, you will never know." He walked over and took Miss Hudson by the hand and led her into the center of the room. He then led her through a few Fox Trot steps without music. He then stopped, thanked Hudson, and faced the group. "As I have repeated ad nauseam, knowing steps means nothing if you can't lead or follow them—as we just did." He then produced a tablet from under one of the cabinets. He hung an 8-1/2 by 11 sheet on the wall. "We will, therefore, have testing according to this schedule. It will determine the ability of you men to lead the steps and for you women to follow. You will be tested with the experienced teachers here at the school starting on Wednesday. This will constitute your final exam. No trainee will graduate without passing this exam."

The thought of working face to face with actual experienced teachers intimidated us all: the way they looked; the way they moved with such confidence on the floor; their posture, their dress, the way they always seemed to have something to say in a crowd.

Bill and I asked the only two remaining women in the training class, Miss Hudson and Miss Cleaver to work with us Monday and Tuesday. Miss Cleaver looked nineteen years old at most. Small and petite, she had a pixie smile that made me feel comfortable, self assured. If Bill or I would forget, or mislead a step her smile would commiserate. Hudson, conversely, would slam to a stop in the middle of the dance floor, throw her hands in the air, point her aquiline nose at the ceiling and pose for a moment. At the end of each session with Bill or I, she never spoke; she merely shook her head and walked off the floor.

On Wednesday, Bill and I arrived early at the studio. Mr. Fox already had a schedule hanging on the door of the training room. He had the trainees and their teacher partners perform the steps to music as he called them out. For each step, he would have the lead role reversed. Men and women would reverse hand and arm positions such that the women trainees would lead and the men trainees would follow. He sat at the end of about a ten-foot-long table and wrote on his note pad.

As before, Bill and I tested first in the program. Bill danced with a young Spanish-descent teacher named Lopez. For the studio she used the name Miss Lapay. Miss Lapay had marvelous posture and poise.

She made Bill actually look good. Unfortunately, she could not make Bill remember all the steps as Fox called them out. She made valiant attempts to "back lead" him through those he did not remember. When it came time to reverse roles, Miss Lapay demonstrated her professionalism. She unmistakably led Bill through steps he had forgoten by brute force. At the end of the 1-1/2 hour session, Mr. Fox, again, said nothing. He requested the band of students standing at the sides of the room to take a fifteen minute break.

When testing resumed, I walked tentatively towards the center of the room. My teacher/test-partner stood waiting for me. Miss Gordon introduced herself. An attractive, tall, large-boned girl, she made my lean frame appear more so. Standing eye to eye with me, also, gave me no height advantage. She seemed pleasant, however, as she introduced herself to me. As we waited for the testing to start, my knees quivered and my thoughts raced: how would I be able to lead this large girl through all the steps—some of which I still were not sure of—and all of which I had never led a stranger. Will I look utterly foolish? I remember comforting myself in the realization that no matter what the outcome, I am about to have the opportunity to dance for an hour or more with an actual Arthur Murray teacher on a one-to-one basis. Something I would not have dreamed possible just four months ago.

When the Tango music started and Mr. Fox called out the first step, I muscled up and pressed forward totally ridged hoping to insure that I could move Miss Gordon (incidentally, the basic technique in leading a partner in the sixties relied much more on physical pressure than bodily position and direction as is taught today). To my surprise, her bodily reaction was minimal. The slightest directional indication resulted in an immediate response in that direction – like pushing against a helium filled balloon: an unqualified pleasure to dance with. As Fox called out the different steps in each dance, at times,

I imagined we danced at an expensive hotel ballroom. "I might as well enjoy the moment. It may never come again," I thought. When I could not remember a step I just repeated the previous.

During testing in Fox Trot, my mind froze for a short period. I could not recall some of the most basic steps. In the Waltz, I led one step with the wrong foot resulting in our stumbling and having to stop temporarily. In Cha-Cha, I allowed our rhythm to become mismatched on several of the steps. Even Bill looked away when I passed him. Miss Gordon, however, throughout all these potentially embarrassing intervals, gave no negative reaction. She merely smiled as if nothing had happened: a veritable princess. On several of these occasions, she squeezed my hand, winked and whispered, "Don't worry, you're doing fine."

When it came her time to lead me, I appreciated even more the hand that fortune had dealt me: undeniably unsure of the women's part in many of the steps, Miss Gordon seemed to have an uncanny ability—by her own body movements—to turn me in the proper direction. Only this got us through many of the steps. How obvious this appeared to all watching—including Mr. Fox—I had no way of knowing. Long before the last step of the last dance ended my mind completely blurred. I remember only the strange smile on Miss Gordon's face and extending my arm to thank her (I wanted to kiss her). Mr. Fox, again, said nothing and merely pointed at Mr. Ford to step forward.

I never could understand Ford. I have to admit it bothered me. I know it frothed Bill. Why did everything come so easily to him? Not just learning the steps, the timing, the movements, the balance in turns, the arm positions which create the style. He said he had never had any dancing experience in his youth—no ballet, no tap, not even jazz or social dancing. Then, what untaught knowledge allowed him always to unconsciously know exactly what to do and how to do it in a stylish manor? Does nature purposefully give gays these uncommon abilities to compensate for the tribulations they endure in everyday life? Or do the Fords of the world merely represent statistically random incidences of natural talent? Whatever the case, Ford waltzed through his examination with Miss McClure as if he had danced with her all his life.

Ex-ballerina Watson, in like fashion had no problem leading and following her somewhat intimidated teacher, Mr. Hopper, through all the steps with style and grace.

Miss Cleaver brought testing back to reality. The problems Bill and I had surfaced again with Miss Cleaver. When she finished, Fox, again, had that expressionless look on his face, but said nothing about her performance. He merely noted that he would hold a meeting at 1 PM (Friday) in the trainee's room.

Bill and I spoke little as we ate lunch that afternoon across the street.

Bill finally broke the silence: "Well, what do you think?" He hesitated for an instant and took another bite of his sandwich. "Do you think we have a chance of passing?"

"You know, Bill, the way we performed, I don't know. Also, I would think they really don't need five more new teachers here," I remember saying. "This is not that big a studio. Certainly, they'll pass Hudson and Ford. After that it's probably between Cleaver and us. He sure took a lot of notes. I'm sure that we'll hear something regarding that."

"Well, I can always go back to Washington and work for my cousin in the lumber business" Bill noted. "I'll be glad not to have to face Fox every day." Bill hesitated for a moment, took a bite out of his sandwich. Two somewhat red eyes looked directly at me. He spoke hesitantly. "I have to say, however, I sure love this stuff, don't you?"

"Yes."

Mr. Fox had moved five chairs into the small conference room for the trainees to sit in a row in the center of the room. He placed a three foot square table in front. When he entered the room, he carefully closed the door and placed a filled box on the table.

Using the table somewhat as a podium, one hand on the table and one hand on his hip, he tilted his head, breathed a deep sigh, and addressed the group:

"I know you may all think that I'm a real prick; and I know that you may all think that I enjoyed making it hard for you; I know you think that I demanded above and beyond the pale that sets the boundaries of what constitutes a reasonable amount of learning for a dance teacher." Fox stopped just for a moment as if to catch his breath. "There are good ballroom dance teachers. There are bad teachers. One thing you will never think is that you did not receive the best training in the Arthur Murray system. Or that you are not the best teachers in that system; for you are. Each one of you five are better trained beginning dance teachers than any others in the system. You will come to realize that. And, I am personally proud of you all."

Fox then pulled five 8 ½ by 11 photographic diploma sheets from the box and handed one to each of the trainees. He then pranced somewhat back to the table and reached into the box again. This time he retrieved a set of five 5 by 3 inch cards and distributed them to the trainees. Each of the white cards contained typed lists starting on one side extending over to the other.

"These are the steps each one of you had some form of trouble with in your testing. I would advise that you keep it in your pocket and make an effort to learn and correct those items you had difficulty with. You are all young and have plenty of time."

Fox returned to the box and this time pulled out five round packages. He acted differently than he had ever before: it appeared as if the innate flamboyance he desperately tried to subdue, now, for just an instance, slipped though his fingers like the wet seeds at the bottom of a pumpkin. He obviously enjoyed the theatrics—his own life-size Mardi-Gras float.

"One thing you must always remember." He paused for a seemingly endless instant assuring everyone's full attention. "At times, in your worst moments, you may do things that make you appear as incorrigible, base or incompetent to your students: you may tramp their toes or teach them a step completely wrong; or, you may insult them with careless words. Or you may forget to call them by their last names." The sound of his voice rose in pitch and intensity and he smiled whimsically. "Oh, they'll forgive you for that." He paused again. "Or, you may forget your place in a routine and cause both of you to look like idiots. They will forgive that also." Now his voice reached its final peak in tone and intensity. "But one thing, they will not forgive professionally or personally; one thing you, as teachers, can never afford to do—is to let them smell your breath!"

With that last remark he opened the box in his hands by biting the plastic covering with his teeth. He quickly sashayed past the teachers sitting at the table and handed each a roll of Lifesaver Mints. He raised both his hands and said with flair, "Welcome to the dance instruction profession."

We all sat quietly for an instant. Starting with Bill, the group started to clap and rise to their feet. Mr. Fox appeared genuinely surprised. He came by and shook hands with each of us individually.

Mr. Fox also announced that starting at 10 PM—after the close of normal business hours—the studio would have a party to honor and introduce the new graduates to the staff.

When teachers at Arthur Murray had a party for themselves they ordinarily did not have it at the studio. They would select a club in town. Maria's on 13th Street was such a venue. It had a night club setting where they could relax and still have the proper music and floor space to enjoy themselves. Parties at the studio could seem too much like work. For the training class graduation, however, introductions would take place. This required less noise than common in a night club setting.

Arthur Murray used parties for the students to focus the purpose of the instructional process—a way to express and utilize the skills they had learned. They made every effort to make them happy, fun and congenial. "'If the parties the studio had for the students were 'happy,'" Fox said, "The parties we have by and for the teachers are 'hysterical!'" I would, with time, learn to agree with him on that.

The present owner of the studio, Lester Frock, introduced the new graduates to the staff. He cited the particular strengths of each of the new teachers. He called up each of the eight existing teachers to the front of the room and had them introduce themselves to the graduates. Other administrative members of the staff also formally met the teachers.

With that formality over, a spiked punch rolled out into the corner of the large ballroom and the party began. The spacious hall with mirrors on two of the walls and the atrium glass on one wall rocked with the sounds of Latin, Western, and swing musical sounds as the teachers partied until 2 in the morning. A perfect setting for a party, chairs and tables sat at one end of the rectangular room close to the stairway on the mid level. Here a refreshment booth sat in the corner. The top of the stairway allowed a panoramic view of the dance floor and tabled area. Guests would often come in and stand at the top of the stairway and just observe.

The relief the trainees felt in making it through the final testing hoop contributed immeasurably to their enjoyment. I, for one, cannot remember a time in my life when I felt so euphoric. Just the realization that I could dance with these professionals on a one to one basis boggled my mind. Fox had spoken correctly. We did receive superior training. All this had happened in less than five months. I enjoyed the next several hours perhaps as much as any in my lifetime.

I danced with every female member of the staff that night—a literal dream come true. In particular, I cornered Katherine Gordon and danced several dances with her until one of the break periods. I thanked her over and over again for her understanding and help in getting me through my final testing.

Having the opportunity over the next several weeks to get to know the teachers at the studio gave me great pleasure. In general, dance teachers as a breed have a high incidence of particular characteristics. My wife and I would joke in later years that they were either gay or heterosexual sex maniacs. I'm sure this satirical interpretation ignores an entire middle portion of the spectrum; and, that most comprised hard-working professionals dedicated to earning a suitable living and providing a product with value to the public.

These varied characteristic were clearly apparent in the mix of teachers at the studio in San Jose:

Bob Fox—perhaps the true definition of the "professional" teacher of dance instructors. Dedicated to excellence and purity in dancing. Charming, debonair and talented but intolerant of those not able or willing to attain excellence. A closet gay—at least in the sixties.

Robert Rodrigues—the other end of the spectrum: the "Latin lover?" Stories of his escapades with both students and teachers abound. An excellent Latin music teacher.

Mary Warren—Outstanding Gold Bar, International style dancer and teacher. Frustrated by her age, however, in not yet having children, evidently her innermost lifetime desire.

Herb Ramires—short, energetic fun-loving teacher. Latin music specialist. Great sense of music and its contribution to life. Openly gay in a humorous tone.

Ernie Strom—middle-aged teacher. The "old pro." International styling in the advanced patterns. If you stayed at the studio as a student long enough, you had lessons with Mr. Strom.

Katherine Gordon—straight as a tool die. As noted, a queen by all measures. A great "smooth" (fox trot, waltz, tango) dance teacher.

Mary Lapay—small, energetic teacher. Great for taking new students and making them into dancers in a short time. Noted for her wit in conversation.

Dan Sparks—approaching middle age. Always struck me as the "king of the road" dance instructor: doing "it" until something better came along. Nothing ever came. Just getting by. Tired. Gay.

Betty Walcott—came from a rough family life. Trouble communicating with teachers or students; looked nice on dance floor though, and had great legs.

I had guessed correctly about one thing: they did not need five new teachers at the San Jose Studio.

We, all five, stayed for a full month at the San Jose Studio. I was assigned only two or three students in that period, as did the rest of us. We practiced, studied new steps, socialized with the teachers and received a minimum salary from the studio. We knew this could not last.

On the fifth week after our graduation, Mr. Mock called Miss Cleaver, Bill and I into his office. The Palo Alto Studio, located about twenty miles up the peninsula and the Sutter Street studio in San Francisco, needed teachers, one each. Mr. Mock offered the three of us the opportunities (they wanted, of course, to keep Hudson and Ford). I offered to accept the opportunity in Palo Alto (I could commute to Palo Alto and still attend school at San Jose State.). Bill asked for the chance at the Sutter Street Studio. Miss Cleaver opted to take her chances at San Jose.

I bid farewell to Bill, something I hated to do. We kept in touch. Very unceremoniously I also bid farewell to the teachers I had just gotten to know at San Jose. Even Mr. Fox seemed sincerely emotional when he shook my hand and said good bye. I hugged Katherine Gordon for almost a full moment and kissed her on the cheek. She squeezed my hand and whispered as only she could, "Don't forget us here."

The studio recommended we take on pseudo names at work. I believe it reflected efforts to separate the teachers' personal lives from that of the students. I chose, "Mr. Warner."

The following weekend, I shined my shoes, got out my Rose Atkins suit again and bought a new tie. Bill David, the owner of the Palo Alto Studio had asked for the applicant to report at 7 PM on Monday. When I walked into the small building on the El Camino Real in the city of Palo Alto, I again had that uncertain feeling. What if he doesn't hire me? Do I sit around and wait for other studios to need teachers? Do I try to go back to San Jose?

Walking up El Camino Real Avenue I came to the doorway marked 970. An Arthur Murray sign hung from a small doorway. A rectangular building sandwiched between a furniture store and a hair salon. Inside the studio doorway, I became immediately impressed by the smallness of this studio compared to San Jose. I looked for the receptionist. After several moments I realized that the studio did not have a receptionist. People darted from room to room. A cacophony of musical sound filled the small entryway to a single main ballroom in the center of a rectangular building. Two of the walls contained small doorways to three practice rooms. The other two walls contained continuous ceiling high mirrors. Next to the entry, the owner had his office.

I stood at the entrance to the ball room looking lost and confused. Finally, a tall man with a mischievous smile, light brown hair and deep-set eyes grabbed my arm.

"Can I help you?"

"Yes. I'm here to apply for the job as dance instructor."

"Oh, yes. Mr. Warner from San Jose, right?"

"That's right."

"Hi, I'm Bill David. Hold on just a moment."

Within moments a buzzer sounded and young men and women converged in the main ballroom.

"We group here after dinner to impart any breaking news on operations." Bill waited for about ten people to finish forming a circle around him. "This is Mr. Warner from San Jose, everybody." With that, he scanned the circle of teachers. Some looked young, some older. All seemed to have that polished, neatly dressed and confident look of experienced teachers. After his quick scan he pointed to a thin, young girl with beautiful blue eyes, dark Elisabeth-Taylor-like eyebrows and a small up-turned nose. Bill David said, "Sandy, come up here in this circle and dance a little West Coast Swing with Mr. Warner. Let's see what he can do."

"Oh my God," I thought.

END CHAPTER 1

Chapter 2

PALO ALTO

WHEN "SANDY" STEPPED FORWARD INTO the center of the circle her long fingers felt cold and moist. Her hand shook. I learned later that Miss Harms worked part time at the studio and worked for Metropolitan Life Insurance Company during the day. Mr. David turned a small dial on the wall and pushed a button. The hall filled with the sound of "King of the Road," a slow west-coast-swing beat.

Dance aficionados will tell you that west coast swing is performed in a "slot." Doing their steps, the couple exchanges positions at the ends of an approximately eight foot long rectangle two feet wide (a dance well suited to a crowded dance floor). The type of dance allowed us to stay within the small circle of teachers -- and Mr. David. Glancing around the circle I could see Mr. Parrot, an older teacher who taught advanced students, standing with his hands on his hips. Joe David, the owner's brother who worked as a teacher, had a peevish smile on his face. I sensed he knew exactly how I felt. Miss Livingston, a trim lady with curly blond hair smiled and looked sympathetically at us as we started to dance. Bill David just stared.

When I have forgotten everything else that Mr. Fox taught us, I will remember his admonitions to "under-perform" our capabilities when trying to impress someone. "Don't try anything difficult or profound -- concentrate on style." For this reason I merely led Miss Harms through the first three steps (the three easiest) of the Bronze Program. I repeated the steps over, and over, and over again.

". . . .*Trailers for sale or rent, Rooms to let fifty cents. No pool, no phone, no pets; ain't got no cigarettes. . . .*"

Sandy, gripping me with one hand, her other arm and long fingers trailing, her lean frame sashayed past me back and forth. Turning at the end of the slot, her body would snap in a graceful and precise whip-like motion. She looked fantastic to me. I wondered, however, what everybody thought about the simplicity of the steps we did (I could have taught them to my dog). But I held fast to what Mr. Fox had said. Sandy's eyes met mine. I knew exactly what she thought: "God, when will he ever tell us to stop?" . . . "*Know every engineer on every train, . . . All the children and all of their names. Every handout in every town. . . .*"\

Finally, Bill David walked over to the wall, pushed the button and the music stopped. The small group clapped politely and I thanked Miss Harms for the dance. Bill made no comment as to our performance. He merely put his arm around our shoulders and said informally, "Come on, let's get a cup of coffee."

Working in Palo Alto created some difficulty with my schooling. It took me about forty minutes to get to work from my room or from school. I did not have many students to start, but had to attend training and instructional sessions during the afternoons when not teaching, for which we received full pay.

After about a month at the Palo Alto Studio, Mr. David decided that I should train to "junior." Junioring pertained to what I had received from Miss Hertz when I took my lessons at the Sutter Street Studio, which now seemed so long ago.

Bill, however, did not approve of my dress. "'Your clothes are too 'baggy.' And, sport jackets just don't get it for creating a professional image.'" He paused as he must have searched deeply into his financial value system. "Tell you what, you go down to Macy's and get yourself two good-quality suits and the studio will pay half the bill. What do you say?" Typical of how Bill ran the studio, everything informal, everything negotiable, everything on a one-to-one personal basis.

The next day I bought three top-of-the-line sharkskin suits, two blue and one tan, (one, I paid for completely) -- the best investment in my teaching career -- though I ate a lot of canned beans that month. I rotated suits every day. I felt different, looked different, and I believe my teaching improved because of my improved self image.

Teachers "junioring" students had one, and only one studio-defined goal: to sell them an additional package of lessons. Their performance depended exclusively on this. I could now look back and see why Miss Hertz seemed so distraught when I left without purchasing additional lessons.

"New students will buy lessons if three factors of their experience are in place: They think they can learn dancing easily; they have had fun; and if they admire their teacher," Bill would often proffer in training class. I wondered at times what the word "admire" referred to (if it referred to how I had felt about Miss Hertz I had serious doubts about my qualifications).

"Junioring" had certain simple but very definite guidelines: keep it simple, don't teach complicated steps; demonstrate much but ask them to perform only the most simple and quickly learned movements. The best exponents of the guidelines could make students feel that they had a special talent for dancing and that they learned quickly. The worst taught too much too fast. Poor exponents foundered on the shoals of "over-instruction." Their students invariably became frustrated and seldom continued with a new program.

I remember my first Juniored student as if it were yesterday. Mary Black looked my opposite. Short, with curly black hair, she rasped as she walked or danced. The stockings on her heavy legs rubbed together with each stride on the dance floor. She never stopped smiling, however, and enjoyed everything about her dancing. I only taught her two steps in swing and two in fox trot. We just danced them repeatedly for the two hours of her lessons. I demonstrated several more advanced steps in tango and rumba but never asked her to attempt them. I proposed the complete bronze program to her and gave her the cost. She merely said, "Sure, that sounds perfect." I never had such an easy junioring student again.

Gale Lofkin loved to dance. She epitomized the aggressive, confident extrovert. Her wide, white-toothed smile seemed always in your face. She had a natural sense of balance. And, she knew instinctively where to place her arms and hands to maintain that balance. With no prior dancing experience she appeared graceful, confident and in perfect balance. In the few hours we had together, she learned everything so quickly I had to introduce advanced steps to maintain her interest. By the second hour of her initial program, people would stop outside the room and peer in admirably. At her last lesson, I proposed a serious advanced program. To my regret she claimed she could not afford it. Whatever it took to "pick her lock," I had missed it.

Betty Furnace answered a newspaper add. Unlike most "walk in" students, she had purchased a five-hour introductory program. She looked down at the floor at our introduction. When I took her hand to dance it shook and felt moist. I tried to get her to look up, but she would simply glance for an instant and then revert to looking down. About thirty years of age, she had brown hair combed straight back, a round face with a mouth that seemed always pursed as if sucking on a straw.

Miss Furnace had trouble following the most basic steps in both the Fox Trot and the Waltz. Not having a commitment on the next hour following our first, I worked with her an additional half an hour. She seemed very appreciative. I asked her if she enjoyed her first lesson. She replied, "Oh yes." She still made no eye contact, however.

On her third lesson, I had finally gotten her to do the basic Fox Trot and Waltz steps. We danced several full dances in a free style manner simply repeating the first two basic steps. The small record player on the table blared out Barbara Streisand singing "People" and "Moonlight Waltz." She had a common difficulty in the Waltz: she would step too soon, ahead of the slow 1-2-3 timing.

During a very slow Fox Trot, to my surprise, she placed her cheek on mine. I could not get myself to pull myself away during the dance. At the start of the Waltz, however, I lifted her chin up and told her that we have to maintain correct posture. She continued to look down and merely answered, "Of course."

On our fourth lesson she had difficulty with a step in Fox Trot. I stayed an extra fifteen minutes with her working on the step. We stayed "over-time" and talked another half hour.

By her final lesson she had improved. She knew all the steps perfectly when I asked her to walk them out as school figures. We reviewed all three steps in the Fox Trot and Waltz. At the end of the hour we sat and went over a continuing program I had proposed. She still had difficulty looking up, glancing up and down repeatedly. She would take the proposal home and "think about it."

At this phase of the process I was obligated to phone for help from Mr. Rodgers who acted analogous to a car dealership closer. "The statistical percentage of people who return to the studio after leaving to 'think about an offering' is about three percent,'" Mr. David would caution. "Once they walk out the door, they're lost."

Mr. Rodgers, however, had a doctor's appointment that day and could not meet with Miss Furnace. Instead, I asked her to join me in the lounge and talk about her "future dancing." I asked her if she had enjoyed the program she had taken. Again, she replied that she had enjoyed it greatly, but that her finances would determine if she could continue or not. I offered to teach her several lessons free reducing her cost by twenty-five percent. She thanked me for that but again repeated that she had to think about it.

With the buzzer ringing in the hall, I realized I had another student waiting. I bid Miss Furnace good bye. Instead of leaving, however, she placed a shaking hand on my arm and for the first time I could remember looked directly into my eyes. Her voice fluctuated in pitch as she spoke: "We have a dance every Saturday night at the Episcopal Church I attend in Palo Alto. Could I invite you this Saturday -- or some other Saturday?"

I could not answer for several seconds. Finally, I informed her that the studio categorically forbids teachers from attending social events with students. She seemed satisfied with that answer and merely replied, "Oh." She dropped her head again, turned and walked quickly out of the room. Her steps clicked on the stairs to the front door. I never saw Miss Furnace again.

After only three months of junioring, I became frustrated and bored with the repetitiveness of the process -- and the rudimentary dance steps. I asked Mr. David if I could revert to teaching. His initial objections faded after examining my junioring performance statistics.

Mrs. Timereck became my first student as an advanced teacher. About sixty five years of age, wealthy and widowed, Mrs. Timereck typified the average female student at Arthur Murray in the sixties. Her width, not a distant fraction of her height, Mrs. Timereck and I made an odd dance couple. With her short legs and round body she did not seem to step: she appeared to roll. When we danced, I wondered if I appeared pushing a wheel barrel.

She had, however, a queen's personality -- a veritable delight to work with. From the first lesson she made it an obvious objective to create a mutual friendship. And, like most of the older students at Arthur Murray in the sixties, she took off weekends, allowing me the time to do my school work. If the studio had a party she never missed it. Since she had been around and taken lessons for many years prior to my arrival, she knew steps I didn't. She never made that an issue. If I worked on something she already knew, she merely considered it a good chance for review: quite a lady.

Bill David called me into the office and closed the door on my second or third week after converting from junioring to an advanced teacher.

"I have a student I am going to turn over to you," he mentioned, as I tentatively approached his desk. "I have spoiled Sheila Cummings over the last two years I have taught her." Bill then picked up a sheet of paper on his desk and looked at it. "I just can't teach her any more. I don't have the time. She comes in for eight hours of lessons a week. She's widowed and loaded." He stopped talking and looked carefully at me -- how I reacted.

"She's pretty advanced, isn't she," I said.

"Of course. That's why you have to be very careful in how you act. You've got to convince her you know more than she does. We can't afford to lose her. If there was any way that I could keep her as a student I would. I'm letting all the other important managerial functions slide because I spend so much time with her."

"What about Mr. Parrot?" I asked. "He's an advanced teacher. Couldn't he take her off your hands?"

"Of course he could. But she can't stand him. It's like two people with similar personalities competing for the title of biggest horse's ass."

"What about Logrin?"

"I've thought about that too," Bill answered starting to smile. "I'm just afraid Bruce might tell her to take her dancing and shove it if she pissed him off. I couldn't afford that."

"So, I'm the sacrificial lamb?"

"Well, it's a good opportunity for you to stay busy if you can handle her." Bill again looked at me to see my reaction.

"Why not," I said, trying to look confident.

"Good. Just remember you have to act professional and try to convince her that you know your gold dancing better than she does."

"One other thing," I said, stopping in the doorway. "She's not going to be happy when you tell her that I will be teaching her, is she?"

"You got that right," Bill said, placing his index fingers on his forehead. "She's in Hawaii this week. I'll tell her when she gets back at the end of the month."

For those not familiar with the bay area, Palo Alto, the home of Stanford University and Hewlett Packard Corporation, rests in the middle of a peninsula stretching from San Francisco north to San Jose in the south. Itself, one of the most affluent communities on the peninsula, it sits cached between other wealthy residential areas such as Menlo Park, Los Gatos, Milbrae and Saratoga. Comprised, in good part, of widowed women whose husbands had worked a lifetime, saved and pared away unnecessary expenses in order to die wealthy – "old money" -- the quintessentially-perfect location for an Arthur Murray studio.

The cold Alaskan-current flows by on one side of the peninsula. The bay borders the other. This entire peninsula now houses "Silicon Valley," (the geographically correct "valley" actually existing only in the southern portion).

In the early sixties, this area had not yet witnessed the first stage of its two-stage population and industrial explosion. In the early seventies the personal computer would come into being. Like a tidal wave, small rectangular buildings would appear along side streets in the peninsula. Inside, women in white coats and chemical-protective plastic caps would work on assembly lines. Real estate prices would soar by factors of two-hundred percent over the decade.

After several decades, however, everyone who had bought a personal computer to operate a small business, write letters, figure their income tax or just appear more important, had done so. A significant (temporary) slow-down resulted. Home prices fell, local unemployment rose, and the influx of people into the bay area showed negative numbers for several years. In the late 80's, however, the Internet came onto the scene like the morning sunrise. If the personal computer created a tidal wave of development in the bay area, the Internet created a Tsunami. The internet catered to a similar demographic as the personal computer. But now every business, family or individual had a valid reason to own a personal computer. And, they could communicate with each other. A "distilled transcendence" engulfed the region that festered and boiled with groundbreaking construction activity. Structures could not be built fast enough to satisfy the need to house the new enterprises formed. Sufficient land could not be obtained at any price. Silicon Valley -- sequestered from the rest of civilization by its unique monolithic densely-situated structures -- had its birth.

In contrast, in the fifties, beautiful prune orchards, canneries and seaside fishing communities flourished along the peninsula from San Francisco to San Jose. On the El Camino Real roadway connecting the two cities -- now the backbone of the computer industry -- only night clubs, motels and small business establishments appeared at small cities on its path.

Teachers at Arthur Murray studios would have private parties in local night clubs. The establishment selected for the event benefited in several ways: first it received the business from the teachers; secondly, they would advertise the event and additional customers would come in to see the teachers doing their own personal "creations." The Palo Alto studio teachers frequented three clubs along the shoreline side of the peninsula: Horkey's in Palo Alto itself; The Satin Doll, in the town of Mountain View; and Francine's in Menlo Park. Here, every Friday and Saturday night after work, starting at 10 PM you could usually find a grouping of the teachers there "extemporizing." Extemporizing involved doing steps not taught: steps created by the teacher him/herself (to the teachers the "school figures" were always considered dull and unimaginative. Only the steps created and demonstrated by the teacher defined his/her talent and were used as criteria to gauge their ultimate dancing abilities).

I would often attend these parties and watch in awe as Bruce Logrin, or Dave Parrot or one of the other teachers would "clear the floor" during a Tango or Paso Doble. Only when the floor became crowded again and the lights dimmed would I forage forth, find a teacher or one of the patrons to dance with. I would often look for Sandy Harms, or one of the training-class teachers.

The teachers at the Palo Alto Studio had somewhat unique characteristics for Arthur Murray employees: very few gays -- only two out of eight male teachers. The rest behaved like sailors on leave: another separation from the norm. Also, they had more older teachers (over 50 percent of the staff was over 35 -- considered ancient for a dance instructor. Most had the usual arrogant belief that only a teacher could dance. This claim to dancing hegemony of teachers over any other group, especially students, I believe, had some basis in fact: in my own experience, having to teach something seems to force one to grasp that subject matter better than any other form of learning mechanism.

In my opinion, Joe David, the owner's brother, had a curious nature. In all honesty, however, perhaps I read this of his personality because I thought that he competed with me for Sandy's attention. He often acted sarcastic about the profession and dancing in general. His attitude toward people also seemed odd for someone in a service type profession. The name he adopted at the studio -- Mr. Raggin, for example, (don't spell it backwards) – I believe he chose in a capricious manner. His brother obviously looked after him. He conversed often with Sandy in the sanctuary of one of the small conference rooms. They would talk on and on and Sandy would giggle spasmodically, continuously (jealousy on my part?). I joined them several times. He never said anything I found amusing. However, he sure could dance.

After several months, Mr. David gave me another assignment. The Veterans Hospital in Palo Alto funded their recovering patients to learn ballroom dancing. As a result, they had a teacher from the studio give a group class once a week for two hours. The first hour they learned steps and the second hour they had a chance to practice them with one of the teachers. The school sent one male teacher to instruct and one female teacher to dance with the patients. Female volunteers from the studio also danced with the patients. I certainly needed the hours.

To my delight, Bill. David chose Sandy to accompany me on trips to the hospital. Patients at the hospital had psychological as well as physical problems. Sandy, as well as some of the teachers and volunteers complained about "inappropriate" contact by some of the patients. I brought it up several times to the group and warned that the lessons would end if it did not stop. They appeared determined to have it stop, but it never did completely.

Therefore, after four or five weeks, several of the teachers would not go back to the hospital. I asked Sandy about it. "Don't worry, I can handle it," she said. "I've taken on worse than that back at the studio." I admired her for that.

On one of our jaunts back to the studio in her Sprite, I asked Sandy if she would go out with me. During one of her stale conversations with Joe David, she had shown an interest in baseball. I suggested we go to the game together on that Friday night in San Francisco. Turns out the Giants played in some other city that night. We went instead to Horkey's night club in Menlo Park. We danced until they closed down at 2 in the morning.

When Sheila Cummings came back from vacation, Mr. David had the onerous task of informing her that he would no longer teach her. Sheila, about 40 years of age, had long black hair parted in the middle (preempting the "flower girls" of the seventies by about five years) that accented her strong, downward-curved nose and thick lips. Her big arms and shoulders framed a full, but flat, curve-less body. "So what am I doing? Am I being farmed out to the pastures to wilt away in the clover?"

"Not at all," Mr. David exclaimed, placing his hand on her shoulder. "Mr. Warner, here, will take you on to bigger and better things than even I could have."

Miss Cummings scanned slowly from my toes to my head. She said nothing for several seconds. Finally, she snapped, "Does he know all the Gold Bar-level dance steps?"

Before Mr. David could answer, I interjected, "I'm learning them."

Miss Cummings shook her head slowly. "And what do I do until you learn them all?"

"We go over your lower-level steps and get them right," I said.

Miss Cummings again shook her head slowly. She now placed her arm around Mr. David's shoulder and whispered, "What else is this going to change?"

"Nothing," Mr. David replied. He then raised his hand and said, "Thank you Mr. Warner," and led Miss Cummings down the hallway and into one of the small practice rooms.

Teaching Sheila Cummings stressed me more than anything I had experienced – including one of Mr. Fox's tests. It improved my own personal dancing abilities, however, more than any other single facet. I talked Parrot into working with me one hour each morning. In recompense he received payment for one of my teaching hours. Each day he would teach me one new step in one of the 8 dances in the Gold Bar program. I would practice it during my spare hours before Miss Cummings' lesson. She came in four days a week for two hours each day. I would teach her one new step each day. Since most of the Gold Bar-level steps required some physical agility and balance I had some advantage because of my younger age. I would have her rehearse the step over and over again. She made it difficult for me when she would ask me to combine the new steps with others in the program.

At times Miss Cummings would stop dancing, throw her hands in the air and look up at the ceiling. Sometimes she would walk out of the room. I always wondered if she walked down to the front office to talk to Mr. David about ending her program with me. She always came back, however, and seemed in a better mood.

Within three months of this accelerated program, I had taught Miss Cummings all the steps of the Gold Bar Program in Waltz,

Fox Trot, Jive, Tango, Rumba, Paso Doble and Samba. I therefore had a teaching knowledge of the steps though I still had difficulty in leading them with another dancer.

The climax of our dancing experience came after five months. Miss Cummings, in order to graduate the Gold Bar Program, would have to dance a routine with me at the Medal Ball. Arthur Murray studios in geographical areas came together to compete at Medal Balls located at some large auditorium with a dance floor. It served as a function to graduate students in a certain level of dancing. Students had the opportunity to demonstrate their dancing abilities in front of a live audience. It also allowed them to mix with and meet students from other studios.

That year the Medal Ball took place at the Jack Tarr Hotel in San Francisco. Studios from San Francisco, San Jose, Palo Alto, Fresno and Oakland all had students graduating some level of dancing.

One full month before the ball, Miss Cummings and I worked on a Tango routine for her graduation requirement. Dick Parrot choreographed it for us (for a fee). We used the old ballad La Cumparisita as the music. Unfortunately, he recommended some of the steps in the beginning part of her program that she knew but I didn't. I had to learn them as we went. If Miss Cummings had a cause to get nasty and aggravated before, she now had a cause celeb: "How can you teach me these steps when you don't know them yourself?" Or, "I ought to transfer to taking my lessons at the Sutter Street Studio. At least there I may get a teacher who knows more than I do."

We mixed in several of the steps that I had taught her previously. Finally, we had a routine put together having a relatively high level of difficulty. It ended with a physically challenging lift, a pivot, and a drop to the floor. Unfortunately, I had considerable difficulty in leading the new steps. Miss Cummings, at times, would back-lead, making them appear uncoordinated. To our benefit, she could, and did, come in for extra lessons. We spent over twenty hours the last week before the ball rehearsing. Mr. David would drop in at times, watch for a few moment, smile and leave. Miss Cummings never returned the smile.

At the hotel the night before the ball I went to Miss Cummings room. I suggested that we go down to the ballroom and practice the routine. "That way we will get the feel of the floor and the neighboring environment." She said nothing for an instant, but then slowly nodded her head.

When we arrived at the ballroom, we found the doors locked. I went to the front desk and asked to speak to the manager. I told him our situation and he smiled. Finally he merely motioned with his hand for me to follow and he walked out of his office to the ballroom and opened the door.

Miss Cummings and I went through our entire routine at least eight times. My legs pained at my knee joints when we finished. She seemed less upset, but still had that condescending attitude. When we said good night the clock in the hallway read 11:30 PM. I told her to sleep in. We would not dance until late in the afternoon.

By noon Miss Cummings appeared at the ballroom watching some of the other performers. The Bronze and Silver level students performed in the morning and early afternoon. Gold and Gold–Bar performed last.

In my rented tuxedo I knocked on Miss Cummings door again at 3 PM. She appeared genuinely nervous. For the first time in our relationship, she said something almost complementary. "You don't look bad in that tuxedo." Quickly, however, her tone changed. "Now, pay attention, don't forget to count to three on that last hesitation before the pivot."

When the announcement came for us to take the floor, I hesitated for a moment and took a deep breath. I looked around at the scores of tables surrounding the dance floor. The huge ballroom had two levels with a stage at one end. The band occupied the stage. On the main floor at least a hundred ten-seat tables formed an oval around the center dancing area. Only one isle led to the floor where the dancers entered and left. A panel of judges sat at a long table at one end of the oval.

When we walked down the long isle to the center of the ballroom, my mind screamed the irony of the situation into my ears. "I don't even know the gold level steps and here I am taking someone into competition in Gold Bar. Miss Cummings smiled for the audience and bowed before the music started. She had been through more of these competitions than I had been to movie theaters.

When the music started, the affected smile on Miss Cummings' face became as fixed as a bronze painting of a circus clown. It occurred to me then that I had never been in this type of a dancing situation before -- where I had to remember a series of exact steps in a row in order for it to match the music.

We started our first step from a posed position with both our right arms in the air looking each other nose to nose, face to face. This position clued me unquestionably as to the first step. After the first step my mind went into a condition of complete blur. Fortunately, because of the many times we had rehearsed the night before in that ball room, the location of certain landmarks in the room seemed to clue me to the next step in the series. Despite that, however, at about the middle of the routine, I realized that we had left out two of the steps in the series. For an instant the edges of the fixed paste-like smile on Miss Cummings' face disappeared. Her lips curled downward as she glared into my eyes.

Of all dance music, Tango has the most structured pattern. In musical terms, it phrases itself in four, four-quarter measures. In layman's terms this relates to sixteen beats. After each sixteen pulses a new phrase starts. And, you had better end an old step pattern and begin a new one after that sixteenth beat. It creates a very dramatic effect. It also creates a continuous potential pitfall for the dancers if they get off the pattern. (Compare this to hustle or two-step music where you can begin or start any step pattern at any time on any beat as long as the music is still playing.)

In our case, I had forgotten two of the sixteen-beat step patterns. Uncorrected, this would have us finish the dance thirty-two beats before the music ended. If I tried to repeat one of the steps to make up for the lost pattern, the repetition would look shallow. I therefore had to fit the forgotten step patterns in somewhere in the dance. Miss Cummings, however, would not expect it. She would expect other steps in the sequence to follow each other.

Coming to the end of a sixteen beat pattern, I tried to glare at her and whisper, "Change". She glared back at me with a questioning look in her eye. When I led the steps we had forgotten rather than the next one in sequence, I could feel her body resisting the direction I had taken. A rough jerk took place in our styling, clearly visible to the audience. Like a good dancer, however, she recovered quickly and followed the steps to its completion -- and with the music.

Miss Cummings, though arrogant, epitomized the quintessential accomplished dancer. Her body, though not curvaceous, also, did not contain excess fat. He straight lines and muscular frame had a masculine appearance, which, from all that I had heard about her, belied her very clear sexual preference. Yet, she could follow any partner with great sensitivity. She could glide with long strides, "pushing off" with her trailing foot, covering great amounts of distance -- particularly beneficial for good smooth-dance performance.

Because of Miss Cummings ability to "move" about the dance floor, we circled the outer perimeter of the oval shaped floor three times. I couldn't help egotistically thinking that *"she couldn't have*

covered that much ground with Mr. David (many years older than I)."
In the middle of the dance I failed to get her high enough in the air
for one of our lift steps. As a result I aborted the lift and lowered her
to the floor prematurely. Again, the glare and the downturn smile.
Fortunately, we did not get off the beat.

Fortuitously, we ended the routine directly in front of the judges
table. The final pattern had a partial lift and a throwing motion
whereby she landed on the floor in a split-leg position. Miraculously,
we ended the routine on the final beat of the music. Her long, sinuous
body arched backward. I stood directly above her. The crowd and the
judges clapped. Miss Cummings rose, bowed -- never breaking her
paste-on smile -- returned to the upright position and threw a kiss
to the audience. I merely bowed, took her hand and walked back up
the aisle to the dressing rooms.

Miss Cummings made no response to me regarding our
performance. When I asked "What do you think?" she said absolutely
nothing. At the end of the walk through the crowd, she stopped
smiling and walked directly through the doors of the women's
dressing room. I went into the men's. I did not have the opportunity
to speak to her again until we sat at our studio's table at the evening
awards ceremony.

At the "Awards Ceremony" the students received their diplomas,
and had their pictures' taken with their teachers. At that time, they
also announced the judges' decisions. Students competed in each
category and each dance. Miss Cummings' routine received a fourth-
place award (out of nine competing studios). She received a small
trophy. Sitting next to Mr. David, as previously, she said nothing
about the routine or about her performance. Nor did Mr.David. He
merely, said, "You looked very elegant out there, dear."

I had feared that as a result of our performance at the Medal Ball, Miss Cummings would discontinue her lessons or demand another teacher. To my surprise she showed up for our scheduled lesson at 2 PM on Monday and said merely, "Well! What do we do now?" I suggested that we should go back over all the Gold Bar steps and work on styling. "Also, there is an Arthur Murray dance competition in six months in Los Angeles you may want to consider entering," She looked at me somewhat furtively, but said nothing.

We practiced only Waltz steps that day.

Sandy Harms also had a student receive a medal at the ball that year. She and her student placed second in the bronze Cha-Cha category.

To celebrate the end to a very stressful period for both of us, we went to a ball game at Candlestick Park in San Francisco. Because of the large crowd we could only get seats in the bleachers in center field. In the first inning the St. Louis Cardinals got a man as far as second base against Juan Marichal pitching for San Francisco. Stan Musial hit a single to center field which would ordinarily score the runner from second base. Willie Mays, however, playing directly below us, threw a ball from center field to home plate as straight as God would make a steel arrow. The umpire called the runner, sliding head first, out. In the sixteenth inning we left the park with the score still zero to zero -- and Juan Marichal still pitching. On the way home we listened on the radio. The Giants won in the eighteenth inning one to nothing. We never forgot that game. I remember everything as if it happened yesterday. Also, I kissed Sandy that night for the first time.

After less than eight months at the Palo Alto Studio, I came to work one afternoon at 1 o'clock to find the doors closed and locked. Red tape hung across the small entry to the studio. A sign merely said, "Closed till further notice." Several of the teachers stood outside the entrance. Even our secretary, Miss Plum, who would have ordinarily informed the teachers and students of the situation, stood in the group looking bewildered. We could hear voices inside, however.

Finally, Bill David poked his head out of the double-door entry. His eyes showed large dark circles. He spoke hesitantly, as is searching for words: "Listen, guys," he said and then stopped for a few seconds "I don't know what is going on here. And I can't talk about it now." Again he stopped. "Please, just go home for now. It may be a day or two. I'll have Judy call each of you when it's time to come back."

A special issue of the Palo Alto Times told us all that evening what Bill David could not: "A student at an Arthur Murray studio in Palo Alto, Rose Funga, 79 years of age, had been brutally killed with a shotgun at about 2 AM the night before. A witness claims to have seen a man resembling her dance instructor, Joe David, getting into a car and driving from the scene."

Bill David missed his estimate for the closure of the studio by a large factor: Miss Plum did not call us back until a week and several days had elapsed. For the next month activity at the studio waned to a crawl. Some students even canceled their contracts for lessons, including one of my own. We saw Bill only spasmodically. He talked with lawyers and went to see his younger brother often. They had Joe David in custody without bail. They gave no motive for the brutal slaying. One of the reporters speculated that the student threatened to reveal an ongoing clandestine relationship with the teacher. Sandy and I, however, always continued to maintain Joe's innocence.

Working at Palo Alto had always created problems with my school work: about one and a half hours on the freeway from San Jose to Palo Alto every day stole valuable time I could have spent studying. My grades proved it. The restricted activity at the studio gave me the final nudge: I returned to the San Jose Studio to see how their situation had progressed. Mr. Stephens, who had just taken over ownership of the studio, offered me a job. I gave Mr. David my two-week's notice.

I felt a great empathy for Bill David: He had obviously wanted so much to provide a protective and beneficial environment for his younger brother -- a responsibility he appeared to willingly accept. He must have felt a great inner pain.

The last week of my work at the Palo Alto Studio passed faster than I would have wished. Saying good-bye to my students and the teachers became very emotional. Even Miss Cummings appeared genuinely distraught. I thanked her for the privilege of teaching her for the last five months. I thanked her for all the memories we shared at the medal ball. And I thanked her for all that I had learned in teaching her. She would now go to the San Francisco Sutter Street Studio, she said. I wished her well with her dancing.

"I will continue to see you -- if you're willing," I told Sandy Harms.

The news about Joe David continued to dominate the media for several weeks in Palo Alto's quiet family-oriented community.

END CHAPTER 2

Chapter 3

SAN JOSE

As NOTED IN CHAPTER ONE, when you walked into the Arthur Murray Studio in San Jose you immediately saw what overabundance it offered as a dancing facility: two ballrooms, six oversized practice rooms, the women's lounge, a generous reception room and party facilities on the lower floor. Having seen many of the other studios at balls and dance competitions, it always appeared to me as the quintessential studio for comfort and facility. I believe it even surpassed the larger Sutter Street Studio in San Francisco in those respects.

Working in San Jose certainly improved my logistics dramatically. It took me five minutes to get from the room I rented across the street from the school library to work every day. I continued to see Sandy Harms at times by taking her to one of the night clubs in Redwood City or Palo Alto. At times she would drive her bug-eyed Sprite down to San Jose and meet me at Maria's on 13th Street.

I enjoyed reuniting with and working with the teachers I had known at San Jose. With nine months of actual teaching experience I felt more confident with the students and with the other teachers. Eric Strom had quit teaching and taken a job at a local newspaper -- the open position I filled. Except for him, everyone else remained.

Al Stephens, who bought the studio from Peter Mock, had a tall comfortably filled body and a boisterous personality. His large toothy smile had a contagious aspect. It forced you to think positive about whatever you were doing.

Stephens brought with him a general manager, Bob Rodgers. Bob had one glass eye, a long face and red-blond hair. He seemed always to look past you. And, he never let adversity faze him. He was always in charge. Mr. Rodgers could dance just enough to do some junioring, but acted primarily as a sales manager.

Mr. Fox had a current training class in session. I could hear the shuffling of feet on the ceiling of the front ballroom in the practice room above. The candidates had the usual disheveled wide-eyed naiveté about their appearance. I had a hard time accepting that I must have looked that way less than a year ago.

My second week back at San Jose I received the single-most precious gift of my teaching career: Mr. Stephens called me into the small ballroom. He stood beside a slim lady with totally white hair about sixty years of age. When I approached, her broad smile had a welcoming quality that warmed our relationship before we formally met. Mr. Rodgers stood next to Mr. Stephens.

"Mrs. Wager, this is Mr. Warner." Stephens said, smiling. "He's going to take you to more advanced dance training." Mrs. Wager had walked in off the street. Mr. Rodgers had juniored her and sold her an entire bronze-level dance program -- a very infrequent occurrence.

In the dance-instruction business, this bridge from the junioring teacher to the program teacher should, hopefully, take place smoothly. If not, the support pilings of the selling process can -- and often does -- collapse. The student invariably becomes enamored with the junioring instructor, and assumes that he/she will receive all their instruction from him/her indefinitely if not forever.

Mrs. Wager, however, reeked with class. She gave no indication of disillusionment. She merely said, "Wonderful, a pleasure to meet you." She had that same smile and welcoming sincerity for everyone she met. And, for whatever foolish reason, in the three years I taught her, her total fidelity towards me or for what I recommended never wavered.

Mrs. Wager had, also, one other irresistible-to-the-studio attribute – money.

From her first lesson I recognized two unmistakable qualities about Edna Wager: her gracious personality; and, her difficulty in learning to dance well. Though she looked elegant with her slim body, carved features, totally white hair and ready smile, she apparently had problems in her joints, preventing her from moving fluently. She, therefore, approached every new step with difficulty and caution.

On my third week at San Jose I received yet another boon to my teaching career: Dorothy Jano had answered an ad in the newspaper advertising free dance lessons. She signed up for an entire bronze program at the first interview.

At our first lesson, I asked her if she was surprised not to be taking lessons from Mr. Rodgers.

"Oh, no! I recognized immediately that he was a salesman," she said smiling. "He had dollar-signs in his eyes -- not dance steps." About the same age as Mrs. Wager, she had a more rounded body and light-brown-dyed hair. Her full body, aquiline nose and more capricious nature made her somewhat the antithesis of Mrs. Wager. The delight she provided as a student came from her irrepressible zeal and *joie de vivre.* A churlish smile, parted to one side, reinforced her "devil may care" personality. Her vocabulary did not contain the word, caution. She would try anything.

Martha Livingston had taken lessons at the San Jose Studio for over 15 years. Though in her eighties, she had advanced to the Gold Bar dance program.

"Mr. Warner, here, has danced Gold Bar in competition at the last Medal Ball," Stephens noted at our introduction the following week.

Mrs. Livingston had a startled look, as if surprised by everyday events taking place. Tall and thin, she had a somewhat cavernous appearance to her face. The wife of a retired lawyer, they lived in the wealthy community of Los Altos. As she frankly admitted, she took dance lessons in order to "keep her arms and legs active." She had severe arthritis problems. She had no problem with my lack of sustained teaching experience. Another plus for me.

Dorothy Kelly completed the list of students that Mr. Stephens could turn over to me. Unlike the three older ladies, Miss Kelly looked about thirty years of age. Short, chunky and boisterous, she approached everything with zeal and optimism.

"Well, where do we start?" She asked on her first lesson.

"Miss Kelly, excuse me but Mr. Rodgers didn't mention anything at our introduction. Where are you in your dancing?"

"I don't know. My boyfriend and I just like to dance at parties. I just want to be able to dance enough to have fun."

Mrs. Wager, Mrs. Jano and Mrs. Livingston typified the students at Arthur Murray in the sixties. In contrast, having attended many parties and having myself taken lessons at Arthur Murray Studios in the 21st Century, I have been amazed at the young ages of the students today -- and the mix of men to women students. In the sixties I would estimate the average age of the women students at about fifty-five. And, as I recall, the mix of women to men students stood at about three to two. (At parties, the men teachers had a very clear assignment -- to dance with as many of the women students as possible in order to counteract this shortfall of men.) Recently, I see very few older students. And, I see more young men at the parties than women.

I believe several cohort-related factors contributed to these demographics: The average age of the adult population in the sixties (those over 21 -- and well above) stood at an all time high. In this construct, women may have survived longer and in greater numbers than men.

Dance studios did not hold proprietary rights to selling procedures. These (now illegal) long-term customer contract arrangements became pervasive throughout many consumer products in the sixties: fitness centers, gymnasiums, dating services and many other businesses freely sold irrevocable lifetime or other long-term membership contracts to their clients. Many would go bankrupt soon thereafter and the customer lost all. To its credit, an Arthur Murray Studio, for all practical purposes, never did that. New owners or another studio would honor the contract. In those days, the attitude of government rested upon the principles of *laissez-faire* (stay out of private business proceedings) and *caveat emptor* (let the buyer beware) -- if you were stupid enough to buy something worthless, you deserved to suffer the consequences.

For several months I had only the four students. Each came in an average of two to three hours a week. I therefore had only about twelve hours of teaching time a week. I received some pay for attending training sessions and business meetings each day, but my finances could not continue at this level indefinitely. My money in the bank had to remain reserved for tuition only.

Fortunately, after five months Mrs. Wager approached completion of her Bronze Program (coming in three days a week she advanced relatively fast). This entitled her to go to the Medal Ball approaching in two months in Sacramento, California. However, her styling and fluidity of motion had not improved much. She agreed to come in for the next two months five days a week. We would prepare a routine and work on her fluidity.

Mrs. Wager opted to dance the Waltz as her demonstration at the ball. She would need to learn a routine in less than two months. We spent our entire lesson time learning the routine for the next two months. Mr. Fox provided some valuable help in matching a routine for her to do that did not require an excess of athletic movements. He did have a marvelous understanding of people and their relative abilities.

"What do you think we should do for the finish?" Mrs. Wager stood outside the doorway looking into the room we used to practice our routine on the third floor.

"I think we should just end with a simple shoulder lift and let you spin and drop to the floor," I answered.

"That sounds easy," she replied.

"It will not be easy to make it look good to the judges in Sacramento," I offered. "They can be pretty tough."

"What do you think about Fox's idea to repeat the pivots after we do the Viennese Waltz step?" Mrs. Wager asked, looking pensive.

"I would not question what he recommends" I answered.

The studio rented a large blazing green bus. Teachers and the students traveled together to Sacramento and all stayed at the Hyatt Hotel. Since I had no other students at the medal ball, I spent the whole evening before talking to Mrs. Wager in the hotel lounge.

"Well, I just came home one night at 5 PM," She noted, holding up her glass as I poured from a bottle of red wine. "The front door was open and our dog Fetch was outside on the front lawn. The living room was bare of some of some of his favorite furniture." She put her glass down as if trying to remember exact details. Her red, pursed lips set off her white hair and clear blue eyes. She began to speak very slowly, tentatively, searching for words. "He didn't even leave his picture. . . . I had it sitting on the dining room table." A small tear about the size of a split green pea began to appear in one eye. "Perhaps he wanted to give it to her."

"You still love him, don't you?" I asked.

Mrs. Wager didn't answer. She nodded her head.

"Why?" I asked. "He doesn't deserve it. Not after acting like that."

"You don't understand."

"I must not."

Mrs. Wager took another sip from her glass and placed her hand on mine. "It's been over five years now. Strange -- for years I couldn't talk about it at all." She paused again as if unsure whether she wanted to proceed or not. "She wasn't what you call -- 'attractive'."

"What do you mean," I countered "'She sure 'attracted' him.'"

"'Yes. . . .but she didn't, what should I say, . . . 'try'.'"

"That's hard to believe."

"It's true." Again, a long pause. "You see! She has cerebral palsy. . . She's in a wheelchair."

I sat staring blankly at Mrs. Wager for several seconds. Now, I started to grope for words. "But!" I said finally. "Why? Why would he. . . ?"

Mrs. Wager, now, also, seemed not able to find the correct words. "That's just the way he. . . . was."

"My God! Are you telling me that he pitied her?"

"It's something like that, I believe."

"But what about you? How could he feel he's doing the right thing leaving you to fend for yourself? Are you telling me that a man

51

would sneak under cover to hold clandestine meetings, disparage the sanctity of his wedding vows and finally abandon his wife of thirty years for a woman, whom, from the start, he felt obligations of pity for?"

Mrs. Wager, now, just raised her hands in an inquisitive gesture. I wanted her to expand on how all this had transpired -- how he knew this woman, how he became so involved as to actually leave her, or if she saw all this coming. But, she seemed so distressed and appeared to regret bringing up the topic that I opted to change the subject. In all the time I knew Mrs. Wager she would never broach the topic of her divorced husband again.

We danced our Waltz routine at the ball the next day in an acceptable manner. We stumbled on one of the steps and failed to execute a planned lift in the middle of the program. We did not place in the top five award slots, but Mrs. Wager did get her Bronze plaque for completion of the program.

When we arrived back in San Jose on Sunday evening Mrs. Wager invited me to have dinner with her and her house-mate. She rented a room in a beautiful home in the Willow Glen section of San Jose. Since we would all eat together I did not consider this a violation of the strict rule Arthur Murray Studios has against teachers fraternizing with students.

Martha Bilda loved to talk. She talked as she prepared dinner; she talked as we ate and she talked as we sat in her living room enjoying a glass of organic grape-juice cider she had made herself. In fact, she loved to talk so much, later, she called me just to repeat local gossip. She had known Edna and Harry long before their divorce. "Mr. Warner, I will never understand what got into that man's head," she would say. "It remains the eighth wonder of the world for me." It's as if he became possessed. I just don't know what he was thinking. But, just how he could do it to Edna I will never know."

"Congratulations on your completion of the bronze program, Mrs. Wager," Bob Rodgers said as he placed a large plastic-covered book on the table. Mr. Stephens looked wide-eyed at her as he clasped his hands and set them on the table. "Do you remember how you said you did not think you could ever finish the Bronze program? Well, look at you now," he said, smiling across the table.

I sat next to Mrs. Wager at the small table in one of the four small rooms with only one door and no windows along one side of the large ballroom. Bob Knight sat across from her. "How do you think Mrs. Wager did on her routine, Mr. Warner," Rodgers asked, smiling broadly.

"She did fine," I answered. "She even added something to the routine at the end we had not choreographed," I continued. Now, Mrs. Wager smiled.

"Did you see the routine, Mr. Fox?" Rodgers asked.

"I did."

"What did you think?"

"I think she looked elegant, particularly, in that red-satin dress." Mr. Fox placed his hand on her shoulder.

"Do you think Mrs. Wager has the potential to go on to silver-category dancing, Mr. Warner?" Mr. Stephens now had his hand on Mrs. Wager's hand.

"I don't see any reason why not," I said.

"Mr. Rodgers, what was your assessment of her dancing?"

"I believe she exhibited a style all of her own -- and looked marvelous." With that last statement Rodgers stood up and walked to small cabinet in the corner of the room and came back with three eight-page 8-1/2 by 11 folders in his hand. He placed them on the table in front of Mrs. Wager.

"Mrs. Wager, these are the listings of the steps of the Silver, Gold and Gold Bar programs in ballroom dancing taught at Arthur Murrays."

Mr. Rodgers began by opening the Silver Medal folder. He pointed to the first page. "As you can see, these ten steps in the Silver have names similar to the names you have done in the Bronze program." he paused for a moment. "For example in the Samba, La Corte, La Cumparisita, etc. etc.'" He then became very serious, "But in the Gold and Gold Bar programs the steps take on an English-international flavor. In this program we move into a whole new realm of dancing. Do you understand what I mean, Mrs. Wager?"

Mrs. Wager sat across the table from Rodgers looking at the long list of names in the booklet. "Yes, I think I do, Mr. Rodgers. I have seen Gold Bar dancers in the competitions at the medal ball. It **is** definitely different."

Mr. Rodgers reached his arm across the table and clasped Mrs. Wagers hand between his own and said softly, almost in a whisper, "We want to make it possible for you to dance like that -- Gold Bar style. Can you imagine how you will feel when you are dancing like some of the performers you saw at the medal ball?"

"It's hard for me to imagine," she replied.

Mr. Stephens now stood up and walked from his end of the table to face Mrs. Wager directly, still standing. "You see, Mrs. Wager, Mr. Rodgers and I spoke about this at length last night. You are special to us and to Mr. Warner, of course, also. Let me just ask you this. Do you take your dancing seriously?"

"I think so," she replied.

"Do you take pride in yourself and in your abilities to accomplish whatever you begin?"

"Of course."

"Do you think that you have courage and the determination to become an accomplished dancer?"

Mrs. Wager hesitated for just an instant. "I would like to think so," she finally replied. (Interesting to note that all three questions asked guaranteed an answer in the affirmative).

Now, Stephens backed away from the table. "Mr. Rodgers, you had better talk to her about this. You know the details and the advantages to her so much better. We are going to be very honest and talk very frankly to you now about finances."

Rodgers opened a small book. He quoted directly: "Mrs. Wager, as you know, the introductory bronze program which you just completed we let you have at the reduced price of $4,475." He stopped for a moment and looked at her reaction. "Just quoting figures, The Silver program of dancing, a more difficult series, normally runs $8,000. The Gold and Gold Bar series $10,000 each."

Stephens broke into Rodgers' presentation: "Mrs. Wager, we -- and Mr. Warner, also -- want you to accomplish your goals in dancing." Before proceeding he referred to the book again. "We also recognize and have had the experience of noting that students do better when they see the whole goal before them and adjust their thinking and their lifestyle to meet that goal."

Now, Rodgers came back. "Trust me Mrs. Wager, I have had to twist his arm on this, but here is what we decided to let you do: The full program through Gold Bar in your dancing career would ordinarily cost you $28,000 – 8,000 for Silver and 10,000 for Gold and Gold Bar each." He waited an instant for Mrs. Wager to do the math in her mind. "If you will guarantee the success of your dancing career this week -- by Friday -- we can let you have the entire program for only $24,900." Mr. Rodgers paused again waiting for her to react. "And, we can allow you to keep your same teacher, Mr. Warner, for the entire program."

Mrs. Wager did not say anything. She looked at me. Then she looked at Fox. Finally, she faced Rodgers and said, only, "That's a lot of money! The house I rent in Willow Glen -- a very nice area -- is not worth that much in real-estate value! I'm not sure I can afford it."

The broad smile melted from Rodgers face. He once more reached across the table, placed the palms of his hands over her knuckles again and said, "Mrs. Wager, you can't afford not to take the offer." He then proceeded to ask the exact three questions again that Stephens had asked at the beginning of the interview for which they had gotten the three affirmative answers: "Do you take your dancing seriously. . . . etc. etc..

Mrs. Wager again answered all questions positively, but this time the smile had left her face. She looked at me and then at Mr. Fox. I don't remember my expression. Mr. Fox nodded his head.

To my surprise, she did not act indecisively. She promptly got up from the table, placed the paper containing the figures Rodgers had given her in her purse, and said with conviction, "I'll let you know by Friday."

I had a lesson with Mrs. Wager that afternoon. We occupied one of the practice rooms on the third floor.

"Well, what did "you' think about that?" she asked on entering the room.

"Mrs. Wager, that's a decision you should make. I do not know your monetary conditions."

"You would not be offended if I did not take the offer?" she asked looking directly at me.

"No, I would not," I replied.

"Well, you see, I have some money that I received from the divorce settlement. Also, land that we both owned in Texas that went up in value and we sold. However, I have to live on it for the rest of my life. I cannot waste it. How do I know that the studio will not go bankrupt before I finish the program in four of five years -- or however long it takes? Isn't that possible?"

I felt guilty about looking her in the eye. "Other studios would honor your purchase," I replied. "But yes, it is possible," I replied. I finally put my hand on her shoulder. "Mrs. Wager, you do whatever you feel comfortable with. If you can't afford it, I would advise you not to do it -- simple as that."

"What would you think if I only purchased the Silver program at this time? Then I could see how things go from there."

"Sure, that makes sense."

When Mrs. Wager had her interview with Rodgers, Stephens and Fox on Friday, I did not receive an invitation to attend. When stating that she would commit to only the Silver program at this time, they, again, went through the three affirmative-response-solicitation questions one more time. Undaunted, however, she reiterated her refusal to purchase the entire program.

This process with Mrs. Wager marked a water-shed event in my teaching at the San Jose Studio: my contacts with and relationships with management never seemed the same. *"Surely, they didn't expect all my students to buy the ultimate of lessons they wanted to sell."* Yet, on the following Monday, Rodgers called me into his office:

"Kelly, Dorothy Kelly, I have some bad news for you." Rodgers looked around the room with his one good eye. He seemed to look past me when he said, "Were going to have Kelly take lessons from Mr. Rodrigues from now on."

"Why?"

"Because she wants to specialize in the Latin dances. As you know, he has extensive knowledge and experience in those dances."

"How did this come about?"

Now Rodgers seemed upset with my further pursuit of the matter. "We interview and take surveys of our students' particular needs and desires from time to time. That's 'how'!"

"I see." I let the information set in for a moment. "How come she never said anything about it to me," I responded.

"Look, I'm not going to sit here and argue with you. I'm telling you she is no longer your student, and that's that. Do you understand?"

I did not answer. I turned and left the room.

The courts set a trial date for Joe. David. His lawyer had requested a change of venue due to speculative media coverage in Palo Alto. Also, they feared that with Palo Alto having such an affluent constituency they might feel prejudiced against an "outsider' of lower financial means. They moved the trial venue to San Jose. From what Sandy read in the papers they had a strong case against him, though she still could not accept that he did it. "I just cannot imagine Joe with a shotgun in his hand killing an old lady." She told me that his lawyers had asked her to testify on his behalf. She declined, however. "What am I going to tell the jury -- that he was a nice guy? I wasn't there that night." She speculated: "Do you think they hope I might make up something to clear him just because I liked him?"

The trial dominated the media in San Jose for several months. Sandy and I sat in on one of the trial sessions. Joe did not acknowledge our presence. He did not look the same. Bill sat in the first row. He evidently paid all the legal fees. Sandy still hoped something would surface that would clear him. As the trial continued, however, that did not happen.

At the studio the storm clouds continued over my teaching career and became darker regardless of which way the wind blew. It was as if I had been air-brushed out of the studio teaching game plan. Several weeks after losing Dorothy Kelly as a student, Dorothy Jano and I sat at a small table during one of the Friday night parties. She leaned over and whispered to me that Rodgers and Stephens had cornered her in one of the small conference rooms the previous day. "They asked such strange questions." She looked around and behind. "Did I like my instruction? Did I like my progress? Did I advance as fast as I thought I would? I told them that in general, yes -- you know I always think I can do better." Suddenly she became serious. "Then, they said, flatly -- without getting my opinion -- that they were going to change my teacher. They said I would progress much faster with a more advanced teacher."

One of the other students came by the table and talked to Dorothy Jano for a moment and left. She continued: "You know me, Mr. Warner. You don't tell me what to do. Besides, I'm happy with what we've done. I don't want to change teachers in the middle of our program. I told them I was thinking about leaving the studio. If they insisted on changing my teacher I'd do it now." She smirked and said, "They all of a sudden became quiet. I thought Rodgers would wet his pants. They said, "'Oh no, that's not necessary. We just wanted you to be happy and progress quickly with your dancing.'"

I asked Mrs. Livingston if Rodgers had talked to her about her dancing and about changing her teacher. She seemed stunned to realize that I would have knowledge of it. "I told them that at my age I would rather not be changing teachers often."

The clouds continued to darken. I just could not understand why. Lightning struck several days later when Mr Rodgers called me into his office. From the moment I received the notice I knew unequivocally why. He seemed nervous and had difficulty speaking clearly. "Warner," he said, clearing his throat. "I don't want you to take this personally. This has nothing to do with your performance or your abilities." He opened the top draw of his desk and removed an 8-1/2 by 11 sheet of paper. He glanced at it for several seconds and then handed it to me. "As you can see, we have eight teachers on the staff here. Unfortunately, we only have a sum total of sixty students. That makes for only a little more than seven students per teacher."

As Rodgers spoke, my mind raced ahead. I could anticipate each exact word before he said it -- exactly what I did not want to hear. I had finally worked it out. Everything had fallen in place: I had the perfect job as far as working hours, location, timing -- and I enjoyed it immensely. I would have to drop out of school and try to get another job. My mind tried to assess what options I had: I could just act polite and ask him to reconsider the numbers; I could work on his sympathy telling him how badly I needed the job; I could tell him I would take a lower pay scale with less students. As I considered each option, the more I realized it had zero chance for success. *"The decision has already been made. He's just carrying out the details."*

I had fought unsuccessfully since early youth the negative personality traits of a timid nature, never saying enough in group gatherings, and giving in too easily. Now, however, I could not go around, under, or over that brick wall at my back. Before Rodgers could say another word I must have reached across the table, placed my hand on his and said simply. "Rodgers, I'm going to continue to come to work here, today, tomorrow and as long as I have students." Pulling his hand back he started to say. "Well, you don't understand, that's what I. . . ." Before he could finish, I grasped his hand again. "No! **You** don't understand. I said I'm coming to work every day." I had to pause. I felt uncomfortable, angry, but scared, unable to breath. "You are going to require the police here every day of every week dragging me out of the building by the heels kicking and screaming," I blurted out in a loud voice. "If you don't believe I'll do it, you can read about it in the newspapers."

Rodgers looked genuinely shocked. And, for more time than I can remember he sat frozen, his good eye glaring across the desk at me. He prepared to say something. The phone on his desk rang, however, interrupting him. He picked it up quickly still maintaining eye contact with me. He just said, "Rodgers." He did not speak. He merely listened, and listened.

When he placed the phone back on the receiver he said nothing for several seconds still staring blankly across the table. Because of his bad eye, I believe, he had a "tongue in cheek" boyish, sort of impish smile that skewed to one side of his face. He looked around the room, then back at me. Without saying a word he merely smiled and motioned with his hand for me to leave the room.

I never mentioned my encounter with Rodgers to anyone except Dorothy Jano -- not even Sandy. I really didn't want it publicized. I felt somewhat ashamed, I guess. Mrs. Jano couldn't get over it. A chain smoker, she laughed so hard she started to cough. "Read about it in the newspapers! Oh, I love that."

It still bothered me. The question remained, "why?"

Teachers at the San Jose Studio could utilize all the facilities of the building for their own personal comfort: they could use all the bathroom facilities; the women could even use the lounge to rest between teaching or training sessions; they could use all the closets and the kitchen facilities for personal reasons. All of the other rooms they could use for teaching purposes.

The owner's office, however, no one could ever use or enter -- except for Stephens or Rodgers. It remained locked. At night, only Stephens's wife cleaned it once a week. Even the regular janitor did not access the "Office." This did not seem extraordinary: certainly, top management has the right to privacy to discuss sensitive issues and to store confidential information.

Depending on my schedule, some days I would go directly from school to work. If I did, I would take my books and store them in the clothes closet while I worked. One evening, about a week after the encounter with Rodgers, I forgot to pick up my books before going home to my apartment. I needed them to do an assignment. I returned to the studio long after closing. Mrs. Stephens' car stood outside on the curb. As I walked up the long steps and into the front doorway I heard her talking on the phone in the owner's office. I walked past the office to the hallway closet.

At the closet, I suddenly heard her talking into the phone. "All, right, all right, I'll go upstairs and look for it. It has to be in one of the practice rooms." With that, I heard her leave the short entry alcove to the office and run up the stairs adjacent the front entry. I had found my books. As I walked past the alcove to the office I noticed the door open. Curiosity overcame me and I peered inside the office doorway. I could hear Mrs. Stephens's footsteps upstairs in one of the practice rooms. She seemed to walk in a circular pattern.

The inside of the large square-shaped office looked like an army's strategic control room. A huge blackboard covered one wall, a pin-cushion board on another. The blackboard listed the names of all the students. Next to each the name a dash separated a listing of the program they should take and an income target. Below each name possible activities might take: trips, competitions, club memberships etc. A long line of filing cabinets lined one wall. Tags on the draws read, students, goals, promotions, results, personal data, etc. . . . I could hear Mrs. Stephens still thrashing around upstairs. She walked into the upper-front practice room.

Stepping inside the office I noted a rectangular panel about 12 inches high and 12 inches deep sitting on a table. Along its three foot long front face, the indentation of round speakers showed behind cloth material. Sixteen buttons spaced about two inches apart along its length protruded from the top of the panel. Each had a number and a label: (1) Main Ballroom, (2) Small Ballroom, (3) women's lounge, (4) practice room 1, upstairs, (5) practice room 2, upstairs, (6) practice room 3, upstairs., (7) Women's bathroom, (8) Men's bathroom (9) practice room 1, downstairs, (10) practice room 2, downstairs, ...etc.

I pushed the button for practice room 1, upstairs. The sound of footsteps boomed into my ears through the speakers on the front of the panel. "Oh my God, I thought, recalling my response to Mrs. Wager several weeks ago when they had attempted to sell her a large dance program: *"If you do not feel comfortable about committing to a large program now I would not advise you to do it."*

The footsteps in the front room overhead now moved toward the hallway. I ran out of the room as I head the footsteps approach the stairs. Instead, however, the stepping sounds changed directions. They paused a moment. Now they hurriedly traced at right angles into the teacher's toilet off the upstairs hallway. I scampered back away from the doorway. At the desk, I pushed button No. 10. I thought I heard running water. Then as clear the distilled water in a glass jar, I heard the toilet flush. Water ran in the sink. As footsteps exited into the upstairs hallway, I snapped the button off, turned and raced out the office, down the hallway and out the front door. I moved down the front steps two at a time.

Inside my car I breathed a deep sigh. I leaned back and smiled. I had suddenly become a lot more informed and a lot wiser.

When I told Sandy about the office visit, she laughed. "Each room is wired? Even the rest rooms? You must be able to hear the toilets flush in both the men's and women's bathrooms. Now that's just plain sick."

Sandy stayed much closer to the Joe David trial than I did. It ended as quickly as it started. Many had expected the jury to stay out for months. They guessed wrong. In 2 days the jury brought back the verdict, "guilty" on all counts, including housebreaking and other lesser crimes -- but most importantly, murder in the first degree. He received life imprisonment. Sandy could not accept it. She even considered visiting him, but never did.

I could not help thinking about Bill again. Sandy and I wanted to visit him just be give him support. We never could find any listing in the Palo Alto or neighboring directories. He must have moved. I believe he bankrupted himself trying to defend Joe unsuccessfully. I couldn't help thinking of the Neil Diamond song "Brother" (he ain't heavy, he's my brother). We never knew of anyone who had any information as to what finally happened to Bill.

I don't recall telling any of my students about the wiring of the rooms -- not even Edna Wager or Dorothy Jano. I'm not proud of that: I could not afford for them to become disenchanted with the studio. They might leave me with less opportunity to support my schooling.

The next three or four months passed rather uneventfully. I continued to not receive new students from Rodgers. Since the ones I had came in almost as often as I asked, I managed to get by financially. Mrs. Wager continued to have trouble with learning new steps and her dancing always appeared stiff and tense. With her slim body, fine features and pure white hair, however, she always looked elegant and took an excellent picture.

Mrs. Jano continued to exhibit animation and exuberance in all her dancing. She learned fast and always seemed to enjoy whatever we did.

Mrs. Livingston had her eighty-first birthday. She did not seem to mind others knowing her age. She had evidently passed over that Rubicon in time where one changes from feeling remiss about others knowing their age to where one now takes pride in it. We had an elaborate birthday party at the studio. After a long arm-bending session, she agreed to learn and perform a foxtrot routine. Watson choreographed it for us. We danced it in the small ballroom that Friday afternoon at the party. Her husband, in one of his rare appearances, came down from Los Altos to see it.

Rodgers and I took divergent routes for the next several months. Passing in the halls, he would only glance as we passed -- at times smile -- and walk on. He had a boyishly-pleasing personality which belied his serious business objectives. I always found it difficult to dislike him.

At the end of the year, just weeks before Christmas, he turned over to me one of Mr. Ford's students, Helen Fenner. Ford had decided to move to Los Angeles. Miss Fenner, a petite, doll-shaped lady in her fifties, had large brown eyes and a very timid nature. She came in and took lessons three times a week, which helped a lot. I had to thank Rodgers for that.

END CHAPTER 3

Chapter 4

MEDAL BALLS

As noted previously, Arthur Murray Studios used Medal Balls as a means to allow students to officially complete a program, focus their learning experience, test their abilities, and demonstrate their talents – and, to promote business. Our region of studios, in Northern California, usually selected a large centrally-located hotel where all the studios could most easily attend. This year, in late October when the Indian summer prevails over the entire area, they had selected the Hyatt Regency Hotel in Sacramento.

Curiously, all four of my students' lesson plans called for them to finish programs and participate at the ball this year: Edna Wager would complete her Silver, Dorothy Jano her Bronze, Helen Fenner her Silver and Martha Livingston her Gold. Fortuitously for me, since I only had the four students, I could bring them in extra hours to finish their programs and learn a routine.

"Mrs. Wager, what dance do you want to perform this year at the Medal Ball?" I asked, as she came in for her Monday lesson. I turned on the 78 rpm disc record player on the table in the corner. Strains of the Frank Sinatra ballad, "My Way," filled the room "What's your favorite dance, Mr. Warner," she replied, taking off her jacket and smiling.

If you ask men what their favorite dance is, nine out of ten will tell you, Tango," I replied, taking her by the arm and leading her into the center of the room to start her lesson by warming up with a slow fox trot. "But you have to think about what you enjoy and do best. It's your program, not mine."

"If we do what you do best, I will do it best also," she replied.

"Mrs. Wager, you have a dignity and a style that epitomizes the Waltz," I suggested.

"I did a Waltz for my bronze." Mrs. Wager stood by the end table in the corner of the room, her hands on her hips. Uncharacteristically, she had a hauteur expression on her face. Her eyes blinked, but she stared straight ahead.

"All right then we'll do a Tango," I said, smiling and leading her into a quick turn step. (I did not prefer having her dance a Tango for her routine. I did not feel confident she could handle the more athletic movements).

"We'll start rehearsing at your lesson on Wednesday. I think that I can get some help in making up a routine for you," I said, resigning myself to the Tango option.

Mrs. Wager had one major factor in her favor – Bob Fox took a particular liking to her -- as did so many other people (her demure "well bred" fourteenth-century aristocratic-like style must have had considerable currency in his value system). This allowed me to successfully request that he choreograph a complete routine for her.

"'No, Mrs. Wager, please do not drag your foot on that flare step. It floats across the floor as if it were 'hovering.'" Mr. Fox may have overestimated her dancing abilities. His patience, however, got him through the first session without losing his perspective of what he thought she could do.

"I want you to come in five days a week to work on this routine for the next month, Mrs. Wager. Can you do that," he asked.

"'Sure, no problem," she answered.

"I'm going to have Mr. Warner work on the steps with me over the next few days," he noted. "Then I want to see the two of you do them for me at the next lesson. That way I can best monitor your progress."

"Thank you so much, Mr. Fox. I do appreciate that very much," Mrs. Wager replied on her way out the studio-room door.

That afternoon, I had finished teaching early. Mr. Fox and I spent three hours working up a routine for Mrs. Wager we both considered within her limits, yet sufficiently difficult to avoid appearing pedestrian. In particular, it included all of the steps she had learned in her Silver Program, two of Fox's favorite tango steps and a lift that I had done with Miss Cummings in Palo Alto.

The entire next week -- as per Fox's suggestion -- we worked only on the two new steps that he had taught me. Both involved a series of pivots and reverse spins which placed the partners in a whirling motion first in one direction and then in the other. Mrs. Wager had considerable difficulty in performing the pivots and spins in a flowing manner. She continued to work on the steps, however, staying after her lesson and practicing in one of the vacant small rooms. By the end of the second week we had at least walked through the entire routine.

Dorothy Jano squashed the butt of a cigarette in a large bowl in the center of the end-table in the corner of the room and walked diagonally to where I stood. She looped the rope belt of her dress with the other hand. She wore a bright yellow sweater. Her large breasts, at her age hanging much lower than she would prefer, bounced as she walked across the room toward me.

"I would like to do an East Coast Swing for my routine at the Medal Ball."

(East Coast Swing refers to the original or "hopping" style dance characterized by vertical-type rocking movements. This differed from the more smooth shuffling-like "gliding" steps of West Coast

Swing). I started to show her a new step I would include in the routine.

"Don't worry about it, Mr. Warner, just do it once. I'll do it behind you and imitate you," the redoubtable Dorothy Jano exclaimed the first day of working on her routine.

"We don't have to do this all in one day," I said, trying to raise the wing flaps on the landing jet airplane. By the third week, however, she had completely learned the routine. "Now all we have to do is to practice it and perfect it. Right, Mr. Warner?"

"Right!"

If you looked for the antithesis of Dorothy Jano you would find Helen Fenner. Shy and unsure of herself, Miss Fenner would never drive down a side street she had not frequented many times in the past.

Early Tuesday morning she walked into practice room 2 on the second floor. Wearing a green dress and sheer blouse to match she resembled an Irish gnome. She did look cute. Her perfectly-round, pert red lips pursed but did not move when I first asked her what dance we should do for her medal routine. Finally, she took a step forward and noted hesitantly in a high pitch, "Why don't we just take all the steps in the silver waltz program and dance them in the order they appear in the folder. That way we would be sure we knew them all."

"We could do that, Miss Fenner," I mused. "But wouldn't you like to learn something new in the process? Also, the judges really like to see a little originality."

"Oh," Mrs. Fenner replied.

"'Look," I replied. "Let me work out something that included every one of the Silver program steps. We can learn that. Then if we feel up to it we will add some original steps that we already have. What do you think of that?"

"That sounds all right," she replied.

Mrs. Livingston left training decisions up to my digression. When she pushed open the narrow door to practice-room 2 several moments late for her I o'clock lesson, she apologized. She wore a brown ankle-length dress and a matching sweater. Her face had a sallow, pale-colored complexion showing anxiety and stress. "My husband has been sick with a touch of pneumonia for several days," she noted. "I'm sorry, but I may have to miss some lessons this week."

"What if we dance a Fox Trot at the Medal Ball, Mrs. Livingston?"

"OK. But, how much time do we have to prepare?"

"A little over a month," I replied.

"I can come in extra hours later to make up for those I miss now. Will that work?"

"You read my mind, Mrs. Livingston. I was just about to suggest that." (With students like her, this job seemed too easy at times).

I saw Sandy Harms again that weekend. We went again to the Satin Doll, a night club in Mountain View, a city just north of San Jose. Several of the teachers from the San Francisco Studio stopped by. We shared experiences -- and dance partners. We stayed until they closed the place at 2.

"Mr. David's lawyer contacted me again," Sandy noted, "wants me to send in a statement for his appeal." I know this bothered her. "I just don't understand. He keeps after me all the time. Like I've told you before, what can I say -- that he was a good dancer, that he loved his mother that he was a nice guy?" She set her Coke down on the table (she wasn't 21 yet). "I always get the feeling that he expects me to come up with something -- or say something that would help his case somehow. Maybe the lawyer thinks I would lie for him."

"That's right," I offered. "He's probably just fishing."

If they thought that Sandy Harms would make up a story that was untrue and witness it before a judge and jury in a court of law, they were betting on the wrong horse.

When we arrived home at her apartment in Redwood City the bell on the Catholic Church on El Camino Real clanged three times. We had planned to go to a ball game in San Francisco on Saturday. "You can sleep on the couch if you like," Sandy suggested, glancing a coy look over her shoulder.

"It's a deal."

One week before the ball, frenzy prevailed at the studio Ignis Fatuus: Mrs. Wager still could not perform the more athletic steps Fox had choreographed.

"I just can't seem to stay with you on the pivots. I know it must appear uneven to observers."

"Let me worry about that Mrs. Wager," I told her. "Just try to keep low. Don't rise up on your toes as we turn."

"You've mentioned it a dozen times. I'm trying. You know that."

"I'm sorry. Don't let it bother you. It just has to fall into place in your mind."

Fox came over to our practice room and spent an entire lesson hour with Mrs. Wager going over technical pointers.

"Hold on to the last beat of the last step in each phrase. It allows the audience to see your final most dramatic position longer. Also, reach with your feet as you step backward. It makes the stride longer and gives a smooth, longer stretch to your step."

"Thank you Mr. Fox. But I just feel like we just don't have enough time for me to learn new ways to do these steps. I don't want to give up. And, I don't want to miss the Medal Ball. What do you think? Perhaps, I better come in several more hours this week."

I needed the extra hours of work. However, these last weeks before the ball I did not have enough hours in the day to teach all the hours my students wanted. I must have taught 60 hours each of the last two weeks before the ball. It certainly helped my finances, but hurt my studies. I had to drop a class at the mid-term cut-off date. It became more and more apparent that if I ever graduated it would take at the very least six years.

The studio rented a bus. All the teachers and students, Stephens, Rodgers and Mrs. Jill, Stephens' secretary, piled in on Saturday morning. We arrived at the Hyatt at about noon. All of the students, I thought, had packed enough clothes to go on a six week cruise to Alaska.

Stephens came back from the registration desk with keys and room numbers for us all. All the students and teachers from the studio had their rooms in a row on one floor. I shared a room with Ruben Rodrigues, one of the "straight" teachers. We all met at 1 PM in the main restaurant for a studio-financed lunch.

We would all meet in the large ballroom at five PM for a social hour followed by a sit-down dinner at six. After dinner, those students receiving bronze medals would perform their routines. On Sunday, starting after breakfast in the same ballroom, the Silver, Gold and Gold Bar students would perform. This would continue the rest of the day through lunch and until five PM. After dinner, the three judges would announce all the results of the competition in all medal categories. Awards would follow.

The last words we spoke standing in the center of the large circle of tables before we did our East Coast Swing, Mrs. Jano whispered, "Don't worry about a thing. This will be fine." I smiled. I couldn't help thinking, *"Shouldn't I be saying that."*

When the music from the loudspeakers blared out a 45 RPM recording of Glen Miller's "In the Mood," the dauntless lady came to life. The audience also came to life. Clapping to the beat of the music, students and teachers sitting on the tables surrounding the ballroom immersed in and shared her ebullience. She failed to perform two break steps while separated in "open" position. And, we did not finish our final step exactly with the music. The abnormalities seemed to have no consequence on her performance, however. The applause continued long after she bowed and left the floor. She enjoyed it all.

Sunday morning, starting at seven AM, we all gathered at our large round table in the main ballroom. Rodgers and Stephens came early. Breakfast came in discreet stages as others arrived. When waiters had removed the last set of dishes from the table, the judges arrived at their table. The master of ceremonies followed. Two dancers left their table and strode with long steps hand in hand to the center in the large donut-like hole in the center of the tables. The needle scratched an instant on the plastic face of the record. The crushing thrusts of the Tango rhythm filled the huge ballroom. The two bodies moved in jagged, but a continuously counterclockwise pattern across the huge opening in the center of the tables.

Mrs. Fenner sat fixed in an almost unconscious state. She wiped he eyes with a handkerchief. The two dancers finished their Tango in front of the judges table with a Media Corte. Next on the program, Mr. Rodrigues' student darted and thrust her way through a Paso Doble Silver-Category Dance looking animated and confident. They finished with the student thrown to the floor in front of our table. Everyone stood and clapped.

I walked over and took Miss Fenner's hand. When she stood, she could not look up. She grasped my hand tightly. I can still remember how cold her hand felt. We walked to the center of the tables and stood side by side. Her large brown eyes finally looked up at me.

She placed her right foot back along the floor for our pose to start the dance.

Miss Fenner had one thing in her favor: in the Waltz, the male partner has almost complete control of the dance. Similar to other "smooth" dances -- such as Fox Trot and Tango -- Arthur Murray, in the sixties, always recommended a strong "body lead" joined at the hip so as to insure that the two partners move as one (this has changed in recent years to preclude possible accusations of sexual harassment. They now recommend a predominantly arm and shoulder lead). Miss Fenners' petite frame allowed me to have almost complete control of our movements. In teachers' jargon, she was literally "a passenger." During the performance, however, the "driver" took a few side streets not on the route. But, notwithstanding these flaws, the routine went reasonably well. When Miss Fenner returned to our table, she actually began to breathe again.

Mrs. Wager did not perform until after the lunch break. When our slot came up in the program, she smiled from across the table. I went over and took her hand. As we walked toward the center of the floor, she whispered, "Don't let me forget to bow and curtsey at the end." Strange that she had thoughts about the end of the performance. I worried about the beginning, the middle and the end: I don't know exactly what happened, but it seems that with four students doing routines I confused Mrs. Livingston's starting steps with Mrs. Wager's. Whatever the case, I led the first two steps of Mrs. Livingston's Fox Trot routine in place of Mrs. Wager's Tango. Since the both dances adhere to a four-quarter-time rhythm (thank God), they have a similarity. However, the number of steps in each measure differed. The result of the mix up caused Mrs. Wager to stumble. I realized immediately what I had done. She looked at me as if she had been at fault. I tried to whisper, "I'm sorry." She did not hear me.

With such an inauspicious start, it became impossible to reestablish her confidence and repair the quality-effect of the performance. Ironically, to the nontechnical observer, it would appear that **she** had made the mistake.

We did manage to perform most of the remaining steps in proper order and technique. However, the overall routine suffered irreparable damage. She did remember to bow at the end. Walking back to our seats, Mr. Fox glanced across the table at me with that Fox-only disdainful look. Actually, of all the people in the room, only he would know what had happened. At the table I tried to explain. She merely said, "Don't worry about it." God bless her for that.

Mrs. Livingston did not perform until just before supper. Her gray hair matched the color of the long, floor-length gown she wore. At her age, she certainly did not revel in performing before an audience. She did it solely to meet the requirements to stay in the program. In addition, doing a Gold Bar routine raised high expectations, which I'm sure she did not feel personally capable of. Consequently, her demeanor and countenance did not exhibit abandon or ebullience, the emotional qualities of the dance she performed. She did smile, however.

When the music started, I could feel her body tense. The first step involved long strides forward and an outside-turn pivot at the end. We thought in planning the dance of performing the most difficult step at the start rather than later in the routine. The pivot actually came off smoothly and in time with the music. This worked to our advantage as we both had more concentration at the beginning of the routine. Though stiff at first, I had no trouble leading her through the first group of steps. At the midpoint we had a series of three "flare" (turning on one foot and trailing the other on the floor) steps scheduled. Mrs. Livingston lost her footing on the first of the flares.

I therefore, abandoned the remaining three flares and did three basic "magic steps" to fill in the space.

Mrs. Livingston finished with a Media Corte (dip type) step at the end. The audience -- certainly aware of her advanced age -- gave her a standing ovation. Of all my dancing performances I remember that one as the most satisfying and rewarding. She walked proudly to the table. Even Bob Knight nodded his head.

After dinner the master of ceremonies announced the results of the judges' scores: Dorothy Jano received a first place in her Bronze Swing competition; Helen Fenner had come in fourth in her Silver Waltz; Edna Wager placed fifth in her Silver Tango routine; and, perhaps because of the limited number of Gold Bar students, Martha Livingston placed third in her Gold Bar Foxtrot competition.

All of the students then received the trophies for completion of their programs while having their pictures taken with their instructors. By 8PM the ceremonies came to a close. After checking out from the hotel, students and teachers drifted randomly into the bus waiting to take them back to San Jose. A much relieved, energetic and expansive group, the sounds of songs like "People" and "Over the Rainbow" filled the confines of the small bus streaking through the night across the moon-lit plains from Sacramento to San Jose.

For dance studios, the week following the Medal Ball analogized the month before Christmas for retailers. If ever students have the momentum, have the proper position in their learning cycle, or have the enthusiasm to purchase additional dance instruction they have it the week following a Medal Ball. Now it became Rodgers turn to perform.

Mrs. Livingston had a lesson scheduled on Monday at 1PM, the first of my students after the Sacramento Medal Ball. The older woman's face had a relaxed look. Her eyes showed bright and clear.

We did not practice steps. We did not learn anything new. We merely danced to waltz, fox trot and tango music on the record player. Probably one of the most enjoyable lesson sessions I have ever had. She had so much class, so much understanding. During the lesson, Rodgers popped his head in to the door of our practice room. "Can I see you both before you leave, Mrs. Livingston?

"Yes, of course."

"Great. I'll be in the small conference room next to the main ballroom." Rodgers smiled and slipped back out the doorway.

"Well, we all know what that is all about, don't we?" Mrs. Livingston had a resigned look on her face, but smiled.

I did not answer. Instead, I nodded my head.

Finishing the lesson we walked down the two flights of stairs to the small conference room. Stephens had joined Rodgers and sat next to him on chairs along the side of the room.

The small office had no windows. It exited into the main ballroom with a small door without glass. Inside the room a small table seating a maximum of four sat in the middle of the room. Two chairs sat along the wall on one side.

Rodgers showed Mrs. Livingston to the chair at the table on the side farthest from the door. I sat next to her. Rodgers and Stephens in the two chairs closest the door. Within moments the door sprung open and Mr. Fox walked in and sat in one of the seats along the wall.

Mr. Rodgers started the conversation. "Mrs. Livingston what are your feelings about the completion of your Gold Bar program and the competition?"

"I'm glad that it's over," she said without hesitation. Rodgers and Stephens laughed while they thumbed through papers on their desk.

"Do you know what's next for you in your training?"

"Not really," she answered. "I thought I would just review all my programs, Bronze, Silver and Gold."

"That would be standing still, Mrs. Livingston. You don't really want to do that, do you?" Rodgers now had a surprised, inquisitive look on his face.

"Of course not." she replied.

"But that's what you would be doing if you did not continue to advance." Rodgers now shuffled the papers on his desk again and finally snatched a 8-1/2 by 11 folder with the picture of a male dancer in a tuxedo and a female dancer in a long evening-gown type skirt. The cover read "INTERNATIONAL STYLING." He pushed the folder across the table. "Mrs. Livingston, this is what will keep your dancing in a continuing learning mode so that you don't stagnate." He hesitated for a moment. "Mr. Fox, why don't you explain this program to Mrs. Livingston?"

Mr. Fox stood up and walked over to a black board mounted on the other side of the small room. "Well, Mrs. Livingston, as you know, you have been with this studio for almost ten years. During that time you have become one of the very few students to complete all through the Gold Bar program." Fox then picked up the folder on the desk. "This program of lessons involves what competitive dancers' term 'International Dancing.' This goes beyond 'social dancing' or even exhibition dancing as you have done at your Medal Balls. Here you will learn a totally new style, a new look and a way of showing off your best features in competition. You will develop an entire new "international" posture as shown by some of the figures in this folder." He handed the folder across the table to Mrs. Livingston. "You will learn a series of routines in all the smooth dances, foxtrot, waltz, tango and even International-Style Rumba. You will make movements, trust me, you have never seen or done before. You will work with me as well as with Mr. Warner on your new styling and routines. Few of our students ever reach this far in their training. You are to be complemented."

Mrs. Livingston did not say anything. She stared blankly ahead. Her hand squeezed on a handkerchief she clutched in her hand.

Fox, looked at Mrs. Livingston directly and merely stated, "Do you now have an understanding of what the program is?" Again, Mrs. Livingston did not respond verbally. She merely nodded her head.

Rodgers took back the folder from Mr. Fox. Jotting down a few notes on a piece of paper, he snapped his head back and looked directly across the table. "Mrs. Livingston, because you have been with the studio so long and because we give our students a special 20% discount this week, this entire program including all the extra hours with Mr. Fox and his choreographed dances will cost you only $35,000. However, this price is for this week, and this week only. I know you take your dancing seriously, Mrs. Livingston. You do want to succeed, don't you?"

Mrs. Livingston did not answer. All of the four men in the room focused on her waiting for an answer.

When she finally spoke, the words came out flat, almost monotone. "'Mr. Rodgers, I am eighty years old. At my age, I don't think I am capable of learning 'a new style.'" She took several deep breaths before proceeding. Her sallow-complexioned face wrinkled in a fleeting smile. "I had hoped to finish my Gold Bar and then merely relax in my dancing -- just dance for the sake of enjoyment -- with my teacher and other students at the parties. That is what I struggled for to reach Gold Bar." After she spoke the room fell silent. When she continued she looked serious again. "Also, in my financial situation I would much prefer to continue to pay for my dance lessons at the end of each month as I take them -- as I have done for the last seven years."

"I think you're being overly modest, Mrs. Livingston," Stephens retorted. "I saw you dance at the Medal Ball. You did great. You were an inspiration to everyone -- especially at your age. You moved better than many half your age." He looked around the room. "What did you think Mr. Fox?"

"Absolutely. I was proud of her. And, I believe she can do anything she sets her mind to do."

Rodgers joined in: "I can't imagine you not wanting to improve in your dancing, Mrs. Livingston. I can't imagine you being a quitter. It's not like you."

Now, all three men focused on Mrs. Livingston. Though some sat, all hovered above her seated in the corner of the room. The incongruity of the mismatch in force of personality -- of youth, age, sex and physical vitality -- made my stomach feel hollow. My mouth felt dry. I could not look at Mrs. Livingston. No one said anything for over twenty or thirty seconds. Backed in the corner of the room, she shifted her position in the seat. No one moved for a full moment.

I had anticipated what would come next. I had hoped, however, that it might somehow pass:

"What do you think, Mr. Warner? Do you feel from your experience with her that Mrs. Livingston is capable of handling international styling? You probably know her capabilities more than anyone. Should she continue her program?" Rodgers leaned back in his chair and placed his hands folded across his chest.

Perhaps the stress, perhaps the indecision, or perhaps just a normal physical reaction -- for whatever reason -- I jolted upright to a standing position at the table. The change in the pocket of my pants jingled. I looked around the table at all four eyes, including Mrs. Livingston focused on me. I remember feeling ashamed that my words echoed so mute, so weak, so inconclusive:

"Well! I have to agree with what has been said." My mind went blank for a moment looking around at the eyes focused on me. "I think Mrs. Livingston certainly is an inspiration to all at any age -- and to me also. And she certainly has the determination to finish anything she sets her mind on."

Without trying to claim a hypocritical self righteousness -- with purely selfish motives -- I made a quick but conclusive evaluation of my tactical position. The strength of my hand, the wild card, the one indomitable weapon in my arsenal to keep my job would never change: it was my students' opinion of and ultimate fidelity towards me (the studio needed my students as much as I needed my job).

When I continued, my voice had firmed somewhat. "I would immensely enjoy working on the international styling program with you Mrs. Livingston. We could learn together. And, if you did decide to take the program, I am sure we would progress well." My voice suddenly felt weak again. "But I want you to do what you feel comfortable with. In either case, I will be proud to be your teacher. And, I'm sure the studio will be proud to have you as a student."

The room fell into silence again for several moments. Finally, Stephens broke the silence by echoing somewhat of what I had said. "Yes, Mrs. Livingston, we all value and respect your personal situation and individual preferences." Stephens stopped talking and hesitated, almost as if waiting for or expecting Rodgers to comment. When no comment came, he made an uncomfortable movement in his chair. The movement acted as a cue for Mrs. Livingston to stand -- followed, in proper courtesy, by all others in the room. She then walked past me and around the table toward the small doorway. "I'll let you know what I decide when I come in for my lesson next week," she said softly as she passed Rodgers standing in the doorway.

Dorothy Jano had her first lesson after the ball on Tuesday. As with Mrs. Livingston, Rodgers requested her to meet him after the lesson. The usual suspects converged in the small office as in a replay of the previous day. The difference in the drama, however, comprised the many ways in which the personalities of Mrs. Jano and Mrs. Livingston differed: for example, when led to sit at the table at the far end of the office Mrs. Jano declined and sat on one of the chairs against the wall. When told what program and what payment plan they proposed, she told them what she wanted, and when she would pay. And when she felt they had talked enough and the meeting had answered all her questions, she walked out the door.

Helen Fenner's Silver program contract for eighty hours of instruction ended with the Medal Ball.

"Miss Fenner, I know you take your dancing very seriously."

"Yes I do, Mr. Rodgers," she answered, her back against the wall sitting up in her chair in the small office. "We want you to reach," he said, extending both his arms towards her spread in a supplicant manner. "Reach beyond yourself, beyond your dreams, beyond your present expectations and visions." Miss Fenner, sitting in the chair, her perfectly round lips pursed into a perfect circle but said nothing.

"You know your Silver Program has been completed with the Medal Ball?"

"Of course."

"How did you like your program?"

"It was fine."

"How did you like your teacher?"

"He was fine, also."

"Did you progress in a manner to meet your expectations?"

"I think so."

"What would you say if I told you that you and your teacher could progress to a level of dancing four or five times its present level -- to an almost semi-professional level?"

"I'd say you've got me confused with someone else," she replied smiling. The small room filled with laughter and Stephens stood, let out a burst of laughter, reached across the table and slapped Rodgers hand in a "high five" gesture.

Rodgers smiled also. But then his countenance suddenly tensed. His long face tilted to the left, his bad eye off to the side, his good eye peering directly into Miss Fenner's eyes. "I'm very serious Miss Fenner." He paused to let the change of mood take effect. "I have seen you dance. You make a very attractive picture. You have rhythm and grace." He paused just a second. "And, I know you have the desire."

Miss Fenner's eyes dropped as Rodgers spoke. Her hands clasped together above her knees, she sat in a pixie-like position. She gave no response to his comments.

Receiving no answer, Rodgers continued: "You need only to break out of yourself. You need only to realize your own potential. You need only to make the one-time decision to jump in with both feet to reach your dreams." Again, Miss Fenner made no reply or gave any other response to what Rodgers had said.

In the clumsy silence, Stephens shifted his sitting position and brought a stack of papers from his briefcase and set them on the table.

"Miss Fenner, this is what Mr. Rodgers is trying to say." He placed one of the sheets from his briefcase in front of the downward-peering, Peter-Pan-like image sitting upright in her seat against the wall.

"This sheet graphically represents our entire dance training universe." He placed his finger over one part of the sheet. "This is where you are now." He moved his finger in a sweeping motion. "'This is a series of training programs that 'ultimate, semi-professional' trained students take.'" He paused again for a few seconds. "Do you see yourself at this point?"

She answered with a short and inconclusive, "Maybe."

"Miss Fenner, I can put you in this class of dancers this week -- and this week only -- for a total, including all instruction, parties, seminars and Medal Ball reservations for less than $35,000."

Again the room filled with a clumsy and vacuous silence. Mr. Fox, sitting on one of the side chairs, stood up and walked over to the table. He placed his two hands on the table and leaned over toward the lady now looking up at him.

"Miss Fenner, I have seen you dance on many occasions. I have, myself, danced with you. I have always been impressed with your appearance and your natural grace. I want you to know that you are much better than you think you are." Stephens and Rodgers now stood and peered down at the diminutive student.

She moved around in her seat so as to sit with her arms on the table. She placed one hand under her chin and the other arm over her eyes. Through the fold in her hand I could see a small tear slide through under the palm of her hand. She continued to look down at the table saying nothing.

"Miss Fenner, are you all right," Stephens asked, looking over the table.

Still, she did not answer. Now, she placed her hands together on her lap and continued looking down. Her eyes had an unmistakable redness.

I placed my hand over her shoulder and gave her a slight but unmistakable nudge. She tuned and buried her face in my chest and moaned almost inaudibly. Her body pulsed rhythmically. After several seconds she whispered, "I can't even begin to afford that."

I believe all in the room heard her. Only the strains of a slow Tango recording in the large ballroom drifting under the crevice at the bottom of the small door interrupted the silence in the room.

After several long seconds, Rodgers suggested that they take up the subject of Miss Fenner's future at her next lesson.

"I don't want to go through a heated selling process with you Miss Wager," I stated in a "private" phone call. She was due in on Thursday. "What financial plan would you feel comfortable with in your dancing program?"

"Oh! Thank you for calling." She said. "I have been thinking about that myself so much this week -- almost scared to come to my lesson. You know me."

"Why don't you think about it and let me know what you would like to do exactly. Call later and let me know."

Mrs. Wager called back that afternoon saying that she would like to contract for exactly one half of the "Gold" dancing program. It had been quoted to her previously at $3,500. It included learning ten new "Gold" level steps in each of eight dances with a maximum of 90 hours of private instruction. "I can handle that much for now," she said.

Instead of waiting for Rodgers to call us down, she went directly to the front office on the way into the studio.

"I would like to purchase and pay for the first half of the Gold dance program."

"Mrs. Wager, I wanted to talk to you about that at the end of your lesson today.

She responded, "I have saved you the trouble. Is the program available?"

"I have a much better program I can offer you, Mrs. Wager. Please sit down."

Mrs. Wager, still standing, walked around the huge oak desk and placed her hand on Rodgers' shoulder. "Mr. Rodgers, I think you and I understand each other. Is the program still available at the price you quoted me or not?"

The young man breathed a deep sigh. The stunned expression on his face finally abated. He leaned back in his seat closed his one good eye and smiled. "Sure," he said. "Do you have your checkbook with you?"

"You know, I just might!"

END CHAPTER 4

Chapter 5

AMALGAMATIONS

MY GRADE POINT AVERAGE AT school suffered due to my mind's preoccupation with studio matters. I rationalized that my total education extended past the pale that formed the boundaries of classroom experience. My teachers did not see it that way. In particular, now a sophomore, I repeated Calculus from my freshman class. "Calculus is nothing more than a simple addition process of finite entities," Professor Clark would say. When I took it for the second time it seemed no more-simple than the first. Fortunately for me, the teacher managed to confound enough of the other students in the class as well. This allowed me to fall within the widened boundaries of a passing area on the curve.

When I took Heat Transfer that year, I had the same experience. I began to question whether an engineering degree had my name on it somewhere or not. My advisor, Dr. Prione, had similar thoughts. "Have you considered changing your major to engineering technician?" He paused for an instant to gauge my reaction. "I have had the opportunity to talk to several of your teachers. Not all of us are cut out to be engineers, you know. We are all different. We all have different interests, values and talents. All have a necessary and proud place in our society." Very eloquent and carefully chosen words -- I thought at the time -- just to tell me that I was stupid. I remember not responding to his question. I thanked the good Dr. for his time and his concern.

With the Medal Balls behind us, my teaching hours dwindled down to less than twenty a week. My budget began to reflect it. My diet followed. To my surprise, I received relief from my least expected source: Rodgers gave me a new student, a young girl of about twenty-two years of age. Joann Lavorne had danced considerably in her lifetime. And, probably had lessons as a child at "Don's Tap & Rap Dance Studio." The extrovert incarnate -- atypical of most beginning Murray students -- she exuded confidence and personality. Her long blond hair, knotted in the back, trailed a long angular jaw and aquiline nose giving her profile a dashing forward thrust. She had the gait of someone about to grab a rope and swing across the canyon, or the first to dash into that burning building.

I wondered what drove her to take lessons. I soon found out: she had just broken off an evidently very serious -- at least in her valuation -- affair with a young man. He evidently had taken extensive dance lessons at some studio and knew all the different Murray dances and steps. She did not. She evidently considered this as one of the reasons he called off the relationship.

In addition to her good looks, personality and self confidence, Miss Lavorne must have had money somewhere: Rodgers stopped by on our fourth private lesson. Floating a trial balloon, he casually proposed extending her introductory lesson plan. Without hesitation, she signed up for a complete $3,500 Bronze and Silver combination program. She also agreed to come in three times a week for two hours of private lessons. Rodgers took me out to dinner that night.

Miss Lavorne stressed me in a different manner: Never having taught anyone younger than myself, I felt uneasy; she always wanted to progress faster than she did; and, did she want different music to dance to? Hard Rock music had just come on the music scene. Did she consider the steps we taught out-dated? Whatever the case, she seemed satisfied; though she continued ask to advance in the program faster than reasonable. Whatever the psychological convolutions involved, with an additional six hours of teaching time in my paycheck each week, my budget and my diet certainly improved.

One month after receiving Joann Lavorne as a student Sandy and I drove back to Redwood City after conducting a dance session at the Veteran's Hospital in Palo Alto.

"Did you read about Mr. David in the paper today or hear it on the radio?" She asked.

"No! What? You know I don't have time to read the newspaper or listen to the radio." I hoped that the harsh sound of my voice did not betray my inner feelings. *"Why did she always have such a preoccupation with, and find news about that man?"*

"He escaped en route being transferred to San Quentin."

"No! You're kidding. No one escapes from San Quentin."

"I'm not sure he arrived at the prison, or was en route. Whatever the case, he's on the loose evidently." She turned and looked out the side window of my car. "I don't feel very comfortable about that."

"Why?"

"Well, I never helped him like he wanted me to. I'm sure he expected that I would."

"I wouldn't worry about that. I'm sure his only concern right now is to stay out of sight."

"I guess."

At the beginning of the next month, a new face appeared at the teacher's daily 1 PM directional meeting. Daniel Gonzales had dark hair, a short, stubby body and a smile that spread across the entire bottom of his pumpkin-shaped face. He became a successful dance instructor in spite of himself. He wore his jovial spirit and rich sense of humor on every feature and personal manner. When he joked about his gay sexuality, even the most conservative found it amusing -- extremely unusual for that period in time. Few could dislike Danny for long.

Mr. Gonzales had made the rounds of the other studios and dance organizations. He had worked in San Francisco, Sacramento and Los Angeles at Arthur Murray studios and in San Jose with Fred Astaire -- the "itinerant" dance instructor. Danny benefited from Arthur Murray's recognition of the growing popularity of Latin dances in America starting in the 1950's. The enterprising Arthur Murray had his trainers hold conventions in Cuba to obtain first hand instruction in the latest Latin styles. The dances he then introduced to America such as Mambo, Rumba, Meringue and Samba became part of the 50's to 70's dancing craze.

To the benefit of my career, amusement and personal enjoyment, over the next two years, Danny became a close friend (platonic, that is) -- a never-ending source of new and unusual steps (particularly, innovative Latin steps), other-studio-war stories and companionship.

Several months later, Rodgers stuck his red head into the doorway of the teacher's training room at our 1 PM meeting. His good eye gleamed as he spoke quickly. A student he held with one hand waited patiently in the hallway.

"Just to let you all know, Mr. Gordani will be coming to the studio in exactly eight weeks from today. He'll come to our meeting at 1 PM that Monday. Start to prepare your students now." He shut the door quietly and left as quickly as he came.

"Who's Gordani?" I asked, leaning over to whisper into Mr. Rodrigues ear sitting next to me.

"My God," he answered, lifting his eyebrows and smiling. "You've never gone through an 'Amalgamation'? How long have you been with Murray's?"

"Going on a year and a half," I answered.

"Where have you been?"

"Just here and at Palo Alto."

"You must have just missed it last year. We do it once every two years."

"Exactly what is it?"

"Look, I can't explain things like that well. I leave that for people like Rodgers. You'll find out soon enough."

That evening, long after the studio had closed at 10PM the lights stayed on. As I left with Danny to go across the street for pizza before going home, we noticed the lights on in the building past eleven o'clock.

The following day as I came to work at 1PM pictures of a small man in a perfectly-tailored wool, pin-striped suit decked the walls in every hallway. Black hair, parted in the middle, appeared pasted on top of a stoic, expressionless oval face. Despite his diminutive height, he always appeared looking in a downward direction at others in the pictures. Others comprised mostly students and their teachers. The calendar year of the event, in bright numbers, spanned diagonally across each picture. Adjacent each set of pictures an abbreviated calendar showed only the eight weeks prior to Mr. Gordanis' scheduled arrival at the studio with the first day showing a diagonal line through it.

"This opportunity only comes every two years," Rodgers said, as he addressed the teachers at the 1 o'clock meeting. He stood by the chalk board. He chalked a list of names on the board. "These are some of the students that we have to reach this year. Every student is fair game. Not a single student -- if they were fortunate enough to qualify -- would not profit from Amalgamation" He paused. "But these students are a must. They need Amalgamation and the studio needs their business. It's as simple as that." The list comprised at least 40 names.

Of my students, only Joann Lavorne and Dorothy Jano appeared on the list. My students had just finished their medal programs and had made commitments to new programs.

"Talk to your students and keep it active on their minds that they might qualify for the program. Obviously, not all can qualify." Rodgers then conducted the usual training and discussion of the status of various students -- the usual business of the day. Before he dismissed the group, he reminded: "We only get this opportunity every two years. We have to make the most of it."

"I always feel so excited during these times," Rodgers would stop students in the hallway. "You've met him before, haven't you Mrs. Burns. Isn't he something else?" The frenzy over Gordanis' arrival heightened over the next six weeks. "What do you think about your chances of becoming amalgamated Miss Lavorne," Stephens asked, interrupting one of our lessons.

"Oh, I don't think I have a chance, Mr. Stephens. I have taken lessons less than three months."

"A lot of it has to do with natural talent. He can discover that more than any person I know. Trust me." He smiled as she walked over to where she stood. "What have you and Mr. Warner worked up to show him?"

"Well, we have practiced a few Tango steps that Mr. Warner says I do particularly well. We will probably go with that." Her large, blue eyes appeared to hold Mr. Stephens in a frozen stance for a moment before he spoke. He then asked if we could do a few of the steps. When we finished he clapped politely."

"Thank you. I'll do my best."

"No, Mr. Stephens, I will not dance for Mr. Gordani." Helen Fenner broke away from our dancing position. Looking down at the floor, she faced Stephens directly as she talked. "If you remember, I qualified last time Mr. Gordani came to the studio two years ago." She hesitated for several seconds. "I was so proud. But, there just was no way that I could afford the program. I thought of every way possible. But, No! There's just no way."

"That's too bad Miss Fenner. But I understand. Have a good lesson," Mr. Stephens called out as he left the room.

"No! No!" Martha Livingston cried out at Mr. Stephens as he stood in the doorway to the small practice room. "At 80 years of age I'm not going to try for that kind of a program. It might be wonderful if I were thirty years younger. But I'm not. So, that's that. I will not consider it."

"Mrs. Livingston, youth is in the mind. Not the body."

"No! That's not entirely true, and you know it."

"I wish you would reconsider."

"You know me, Mr. Warner. I'm a ham. I'm not going to miss the chance to prepare a routine, be evaluated, and show off in front of a crowd." Dorothy Jano responded when I asked if she would dance for Mr. Gordani. "But I went through that two years ago. I'm not going to become Amalgamated. I know what I want out of my dancing. And I don't need any special program to tell me how to get it." She stopped talking for a moment, took a drag on her cigarette. Her face took on a whimsical smile. "Maybe I should ask Gordani to dance with me after I finish. Then we would know if the little twerp actually can dance or not."

The day before Gordanis' arrival, the studio had the floors buffered. A young Hispanic-looking man appeared outside all the windows at one time or another with a rag and a squeegee in his hand. A banner spanned the front entrance to the main ballroom reading, "Welcome Mr. Gordani." All the mirrors in the main ballroom had red, white and blue paper bands draped over their tops as the ball parks do at a World Series game. Rodgers and Stephens ran about the studio talking quickly in short, staccato sentences to students in the halls. They would break into all the practice rooms and make small talk with the students practicing.

Dorothy Jano and I sat at one of the booths adjacent the large ballroom. She smoked a cigarette and blew small circles in the air. Looking at the dancers in the ballroom she smiled. She had a way of coughing and laughing at the same time. I never could decide if the cough caused the laugh or the laugh caused the cough. Whatever the biological explanation, it never seemed to bother her. She just shook it off.

Teachers and their partners traversed the large hall in the standard counterclockwise direction. They stopped often to correct or adjust a step or a particular movement. All had serious expression on their face. Stephens and Rodgers would come by, stop a couple at full speed in their dance pattern, make suggestions or simply complement them. Jerking away, as if to utilize themselves to their maximum effect, they would literally run to speak to someone else.

After one cup of coffee and two cigarettes, Miss Jano and I stood up, found the least populated spot on the large dance floor, and practiced our Cha-Cha routine. Stephens stopped by, but didn't stop us. He merely raised his thumb in the air. Miss Jano looked at me, smiled and nodded her head. In all truthfulness, she did have a natural "joie de vivre" that made all her rhythm dances look animated and exciting.

At 6PM the studio had canceled all scheduled lessons. The main ballroom, its decorations complete, lit up with all its recessed spotlights. A live five-piece band started to play the now familiar distinct Tango, Rumba and Cha-Cha rhythms of the day: La Cumparisita, Tequila. The students started to gather on the balcony. Some drifted down and sat at the tables located on one side of the hall. The remaining students (or guests or teachers) stood against the mirrors on the other three walls of the large ballroom.

After giving the crowd time to settle, Stephens walked to the center of the ballroom with a portable microphone in his hand:

"Ladies and gentlemen, thank you all for coming tonight." He went on to remind everyone of Gordanis' arrival tomorrow and asked all the candidates for the Amalgamation program to note the schedule for their routines taking place over the next four days. "They're all posted in the hallways. I now have a special treat for you." He paused, building the expectation. "We have with us tonight a very special group of dancers. These few have been selected from our cadre of participants in the Arthur Murray Amalgamations Program. These six students and teacher couples will perform for you four dances: Tango, Rumba, Samba and the Cha-Cha."

The recessed lights around the side of the hall darkened leaving only the light above the center of the floor. In order, the couples traversed the perimeter of the ballroom counter-clockwise for the Tango, Rumba and Samba. The Cha-Cha dancers contained themselves within one of six slots nested in an area at the center of the room. The band alternately played complete compositions of Tango, Rumba, Samba and Cha-Cha. The crowd applauded at the end of each dance.

Stephens again walked to the center of the ball room and asked the crowd what they thought of the dancers. This time the applause had more conviction. "Aren't they something?" he shouted. He then invited all to enter the floor and dance. "Let the party begin."

Teachers probably worked harder at student parties than on their lessons, training sessions or interviews combined. And, they received no pay for it. But I have to admit that I enjoyed those hours more than any others in my schedule -- except, of course -- teacher parties. To drift for hours from one student to another asking them to dance -- and, certainly, never being turned down -- not only framed the teachers self confidence in concrete, but mastered his ability to lead an unfamiliar dance patter. Something you could not purchase at any price. Something I had never dreamed possible just months ago

The workday began on the following afternoon at 1 PM in the usual manner. It was obvious, however, that Stephens, Rodgers, and secretary Dixon had come in much earlier. Now, balloons hung from the posts alongside the front door and on handrails in the hallways. The janitors had rebuffed the floors one more time. Fresh, new signs welcomed Mr. Gorbani scheduled to arrive at 2 PM.

The limousine drifted slowly, carefully. The driver listened for the sound of the wire feelers to make contact with the curb. It stopped directly in front of the studio. A dark-suited man slammed on the emergency brake, ran across the front of the car and opened the back door. Gorbani stepped out. His small eyes stood not much higher than the top of the limousine. He rotated his head slowly a full 360 degrees. The driver handed him a large leather briefcase.

Before Gorbani could start his climb up the long concrete steps to the front entrance, Rodgers and Stephens ran down to meet him. They shook hands. Rodgers took his briefcase. They ascended the steps together.

Inside the entrance, all of the studio teachers waited to greet the Amalgamations aficionado. The black, pin-striped suit Gorbani wore matched his hair and pale complexion. Greeting the teachers, he said absolutely nothing. He shook hands, looked disdainfully at each and progressed to the next in line. In the hallways he would stop to shake the hand of a student, tilt his head back enough to look through his bifocal glasses, nod his head and move on.

By 4 PM some of the students and teachers had already gathered to practice their routines. Joann Lavorne would perform at approximately 6 PM, according to her order on the list on the bulletin board at the entrance. Gorbani had confined himself somewhere. No one had seen him since his much celebrated entry into the building at 2 PM.

At exactly 5 PM the Amalgamation trials officially began: the prospective students stood against the mirror on the right side of the large ballroom. Gorbani appeared on the balcony at the entrance to the large ballroom accompanied by Rodgers and Stephens. An instant silence gripped the students and teachers lined up on one of the mirrored sides of the large ballroom. He walked slowly down the stairs and mounted a raised platform about six-foot square located against the mirrored wall opposite the students. He sat at a table having only a list of students, a folder of evaluation sheets, a stop watch, and a pitcher of water. The watch in one hand, a pen in the other, he tilted his head back and scanned the students and teachers lined up on the far side of the ballroom. Without saying a word, he swirled his arm in a circular motion as if to officially pronounce the time for the 'games to begin.'

The first candidate, one of Mr. Rodrigues' students, broke the continuing reverent silence with a rousing Mambo. The syncopated beats of Malaguena filled the ballroom. The two bodies snapped and twisted in a very small circular area in the center of the ballroom.

Spotlights went off and on. (Mr. Rodrigues could certainly bring out the best of students in the Latin dances). When the music stopped, Gorbani almost smiled. He caught himself in time, however, and merely nodded his head. He wrote for the next minute or two on one of the sheets. In a rare example of his verbal-rhetoric inclinations, he exclaimed, "Thank you," and motioned again with his right hand. Mr. Rodrigues' student bowed courteously and walked off the floor.

The next candidate, one of Miss Hudson's students, did a Silver category Tango routine. Miss Hudson could dance with -- and in some dances -- better than the best. Her student could not. He started off badly by beginning the routine in the middle of a measure of music instead of at the beginning. After that inauspicious start the routine only got worse. In all fairness to their effort, (as mentioned previously) a male professional/female student combination has an unquestionable advantage over a male student/female teacher combination -- particularly in the smooth dances. Here, a strong lead by the male teacher can compensate for the student's lack of experience. In this case, the student unmistakably left out some of the routine's steps. As much as Hudson clearly tried to "back-lead" him into the correct steps and techniques, he could not as much end the routine when the music stopped.

Mr. Gorbani, however, showed no reaction to the performance. He merely thanked the student for his performance and rolled his finger in the air.

When it came time for Miss Lavorne's routine, she, ahead of my cue, took my hand and led us to the far end of the ballroom. When the music started, we did a series of pivots in the prescribed counter-clockwise direction around the ballroom. She did a series of dip steps whereby her legs extended out in a perfectly formed bridge, her neck in a straight line bent backwards and in line with her body. Though relatively simple steps, she held each position to its maximum length.

We finished with a spiral turn and media-corte-drop combination (thanks to Mr. Fox).

I felt good about the finish. and good about the routine. I thought I saw Mr. Gorbani almost smile again. Again, he merely thanked us and motioned for the next candidate and teacher to present.

Other than judging Amalgamation candidates and appearing at random but sparse instances, we never saw Gorbani. He did not address groups of teachers or students. He did not have conferences with students. He did not appear in the hallways, ballrooms or practice rooms except en-route to a judging presentation. For the entire three days of his stay at the studio, I saw him only three times -- for my presentations with Joann Lavorne and Dorothy Jano, and when I passed him in the hallway once.

Dorothy Jano performed late Tuesday evening -- one of the last presentations. Her Mambo had all the positive qualities you look for in a student presentation: rhythm, animation and abandon, She had so much abandon that she either forgot or decided to alter several of the steps we had planned. It had no effect on her presentation. The crowd gave her a rousing applause. Again Gorbanis' lips parted somewhat. Dorothy Jano's wide, smoke-stained toothy smile assured me that she enjoyed it also.

On Wednesday, Gorbani, Rodgers and Stephens met with the Amalgamation-candidate students and their teachers in private. The three sat behind a long table in the recessed front small ballroom. The students and teachers sat together across the table. Gorbani never looked more stern, cold, somber. He never spoke in a more official manner, selecting each word after much deliberation, as if placing great import on each verbal phrase:

"Miss Lavorne, I want to first ask you what you thought of your dancing. . . . I want to ask you how you felt as you danced. . . . "Did you feel nervous at all?"

"I thought I did well, though I could have done better. In the beginning I missed that one flare step. I felt fine. I enjoyed it. I really don't get nervous."

"Miss Lavorne, I want you to work on one thing." He stood and walked to our side of the table. "Mr. Warner, would you please take Miss Lavorne in the dance position." He then placed his hand under her chin. Pulling the jaw, he tilted her head back and to the side. "I want to see just a little more backward angle to your head posture. Do you understand what I mean?"

"Oh, yes, Mr. Gorbani, Mr. Warner and I have worked on that often. I am sure we can do more with it."

For the first time, now, Gorbani smiled as he walked back to his seat. "I'm sure you will."

He became very serious. For just a moment he neither spoke nor looked up from the table. He finally grasped a set of papers from out of his briefcase and spread them on his desk. He looked through the bottom of his bifocals at the young student.

Again he spoke deliberately: "Miss Lavorne, I had to grade you a six out of ten for posture and positioning." He stopped talking and shuffled the papers arranging them in order. Miss Lavorne looked down at the desk.

Gorbani reached over the table and placed his hand over the hand of the young student. A parental smile faintly stretched his lips. "In animation, however, I was able to rate you at nine out of ten." He shuffled papers again. "And in styling, I graded you a full ten, something I seldom do." He picked up the last two sets of papers. "In school figures and rhythm I graded you eight out of ten in both."

Miss Lavorne looked up intently at Gorbani as he spoke. He wrote with a pencil on his pad of paper. Looking at all in the room in a slow, systematic perusal, he said with a tone having both authority and conviction, "I am satisfied that we have Miss Lavorne as an Amalgamated student."

Rodgers and Stephens sprang up from their seats, beaming toothy smiles, clapping and reaching out to shake Miss Lavorne's hand. I smiled and offered my hand also. She gave me a hug. "Oh! I knew I could do it," she said, now standing up at the side of the table.

Gorbanis' face, conversely, returned to its stoic, disdainful expression, his small eyes again partially closed. Like a marionette, he gathered up his papers, slammed closed his briefcase, stood and extended his hand towards Miss Lavorne. He shook once and nodded his head. He turned. His leather heels clicked on the wood floor as he strode quickly across the small ballroom floor up the stairs and disappeared down the long hallway.

Sitting down, Rodgers and Stephens now took the seats on the other side of the table vacated by Gorbani. They both sat and said nothing for an instant as Rodgers opened a folder and set it on the table.

Miss Lavorne, do you know what it means to become an Amalgamated student?" Rodgers asked.

"I have an idea. But I'm not really sure," She answered.

`Well, literally, amalgamation means to intermix or to unite. The Amalgamation program allows us to take the best of the International, American and Acrobatic dancing styles and combines them in one. We still teach Bronze, Silver and Gold dance-step programs, but the steps now intertwine the above three styles. It obviously raises the difficulty. We teach the Gold and Silver medal styling in with the Bronze -- if the student can handle it. This makes the Amalgamated student a hierarchical level above other ballroom dancers regardless of their medal level. They can be immediately recognized in any dancing group.

Rodgers looked at Miss Lavorne and smiled. "Do you have a better idea of what we are talking about here?"

"I think I do."

"This program requires the studio to provide teachers trained in the Amalgamation methods with a level of teaching experience up to the gold medal level for the Amalgamations students. We therefore have to make commitments for teacher training and hiring to meet these requirements. The studio, therefore, in turn, requires that the student make a commitment to the program as a single unit. Does that make sense?"

"Yes, that seems reasonable," Miss Lavorne replied.

Rodgers then took a 8-1/2 by 11 sheet of paper and placed it on the desk in front of the young lady.

"Miss Lavorne, you are now only on your Bronze medal program. Therefore, you still have a long way to go. This is what we do for you to get you through your entire amalgamated program." Rodgers noted, pointing to a line at the bottom of the sheet. "These figures are good for today only."

The young lady looked at the sheet several seconds. "Fifteen-thousand dollars is a lot of money, Mr. Rodgers."

"Yes it is. But the Amalgamations Program is a lot of program. Don't you think so, Miss Lavorne?"

"I guess so."

"Is your dancing worth it?"

Miss Lavorne did not answer Rodgers. She looked around the room, took a deep breath. She looked at Rodgers, Stephens and then at me. "Aw! What the hell. I can afford it -- thank God," she said. She grabbed the pen out of Rodgers hand and signed the contract at the bottom of the sheet of paper quicker than I could return my lips from a pursed position.

"I know that you're going to love this program. It's made for students like you," Stephens noted.

All four stood up and shook hands. Miss Lavorne had become an Amalgamated student.

Mrs. Jano would have none of it. "I did my dancing. I am not going through that again. Tell them I am out of town until next week. By that time Gorbani will be long gone."

"Did you pass the Amalgamations requirements several years ago, Mrs. Jano?"

"I certainly did."

"Good for you."

Mrs. Jano did not continue the conversation. Instead, she took a dance position and we started our lesson.

Mr. Gorbani left on Thursday as furtively and as inconspicuously as he had arrived and moved about the studio. At five PM, a limousine pulled up in front of the studio. Rodgers and Stephens carried his baggage down to the curb, but I never saw him or said good-by to him. He had amalgamated a total of seven students.

Sandy had a problem with my teaching of Miss Lavorne. On one occasion, I had to cancel a date (we had had to hold a special practice session in preparation for her Amalgamations candidacy). She also had to wait once when she came to visit me at the studio while I worked with Miss Lavorne on one of her routines. It caused a conflict. After that when we went out, our evening went badly.

As much as I tried to explain, it seems she could not understand that to me Joann Lavorne was no different than any of my other students. No matter what I said, it did not seem to lesson her concern.

She came down to the studio less often to see me. I also found it more difficult to date her on a regular basis.

Danny Gonzales and I left the studio early following Gorbanis' departure on Thursday. We went directly across the street to the Pizza Palace and had supper at about seven o'clock. Relieved over ending Amalgamation's week, we each had a beer with dinner. Still early in the evening for dance teachers, at about nine, Danny suggested we celebrate Gormani' departure at Maria's night club on Thirteenth Street.

Maria's, a long standing tradition in San Jose, acquired its acclaim by having the best Latin music in town. When we arrived the band had not yet started playing, but we could not find an empty table. We sat at the bar. I had a soft drink. Danny probably ordered a Martini. As we talked, as common in most clubs, the noise grew louder as the evening progressed. I suggested that we leave around eleven. Danny, however, seemed in rare spirits. He suggested, instead, we ask two girls sitting alone at a table in the corner to dance. In deference to Sandy I declined.

When Danny ordered another drink, for the first time, I noticed how much he had already drank. I worried about his driving home. Now about midnight, a table became available in the corner of the room. Danny wobbled as we scooted across the floor. He slammed down at the table. I had never seen him drink this much. He started talking loud. A wide grin never left his face -- not even when he ordered another drink.

Danny started talking and laughing at the same time. At the end of each phrase he would emit a cackling-laughing-choking sound from deep in his chest. His round face and long black hair rocked back and forth. He paused a lot between words, but they still came out clear and distinct. His rare sense of humor, center stage, he appeared determined to unload harbored insights. The topic reverted to the studio: "And, what if Hudson did one of those fancy-ass spin-turns she learned in ballet and got her heels caught in a crack in the floor." He took another sip. "And my good friend Fox: try to imagine him in his custom-tailored tuxedo standing on a freeway ramp with a sign asking for cash." He answered each statement with a synonymous sounding cackle that echoed through the small, densely-populated building.

Danny finished his drink and slammed his fist on the table. "Hey! That Gorbani guy. No! that takes the cake. . . . This deity incarnate. This walking God. This human untouchable." Danny laughed so hard his elbow slipped off the narrow table. "What if they fished that dude out of a drunk tank at a local police station?" Another long, sustained cackle. . . . "Hey! They give him a bath, shave and a haircut, buy him a 500 dollar suit, teach him the magic step, and you got a dance amalgamator." He pulled on my arm twisting it so hard that I had to pull it out of his grasp. "Think about it .He never says much. . . . He never does anything. . . . He never dances. . . . I wouldn't be surprised if he didn't know a good Tango from the Arkansas chicken scratch."

"He must know something," I said, trying to stand and get Danny to consider going home (I would drive his car). "He's been around to a lot of studios."

"And sold a lot of dance programs."

"Of course."

"Tell me something," Danny began to have to slow down even more -- searching for words. Some came out slurred. "Tell me, have you ever had a studin try out for Amalgamaion an nod be accebted?"

"No," I answered. "But I've only had one student try out."

"Well", Danny responded, "I've had several. By some miracle, they all pazzed." He started laughing again so hard he spilled his drink. . . . "I thing my dog would pass."

I tried to get Danny to sit up in his seat. "I think we better go. They want to close this place."

"You god it, my friend."

The Amalgamations program fit Miss Lavorne like an expensive shoe: She thrived on challenge, she thrived on achievement, and she particularly enjoyed having a competitive advantage over the other students. And, she evidently could afford the program financially.

Now, Miss Lavorne came in at least three times a week, sometimes for several hours of lessons. She worked with Fox also. Progressing in her dancing exceedingly fast, she served as a marquee exemplifying (to other students) the Amalgamations program. All this gave me a personal feeling of justification and satisfaction. It also greatly benefited my standing with management. Rodgers, in fact, gave me yet another very active student, Mrs. Mary Newbold. With the acquisition of Mrs. Newbold as a student, I had enough hours to comfortably pay my bills, tuition, food and other necessities.

On the negative side, my activities with Joann Lavorne continued to drive a wedge between Sandy and myself. I could understand her misgivings: Perhaps because I taught her so many hours a week; and I danced with her often at the student parties, some of which combined with the Palo Alto Studio. Also, she purchased a weekend party package at Lake Tahoe gambling resort with her teacher as part of a group. We therefore spent most of the daytime together. In addition, Miss Lavorne may have suffered -- at least temporarily -- from "dance-teacher-admiration" syndrome (a malady other women can probably sense instinctively).

Despite Sandy's concerns, I had no designs on the fair-featured and curvaceous young student. Oh sure, I felt biologically aroused -- particularly in the body-lead dance position. And certainly, I enjoyed the sparkle of her pale-blue eyes. However, I had come much too close to losing my job once already.

In addition, for all her beauty, the young lady was far too "full of herself." I did not want to start anything I could not finish. At an age where I thought seriously about starting a family, I could not see her in that role -- not as the mother of my children. I wanted them to have more. For all the reasons above, I always -- and only -- saw my hard-to-understand-at-times young lady from Redwood City in that prospective role.

END CHAPTER 5

Chapter 6

9 LIVES

As an immediate consequence of Joann Lavorne's purchase of the total Amalgamation program during Mr. Gobanis' sojourn at the studio, my assessment by management rose from that of a sand-pile to what one might call a low-level mound: I had not hit a "grand slam" or a "walk-off-the-field" home run in the bottom of the ninth inning, but I had, at the very least, driven in a run with a sacrifice fly. Rodgers and Stephens would actually smile at times passing in the hallway. And, as quid-pro-quo, perhaps, I received two new Gold Bar level students to teach -- Dorothy Huff and Mary Newbold (students needing a new instructor as a result of Mr. King's departure from the studio several months prior).

In preparation for my first lesson with Mrs. Huff, I came in early and practiced one of the Gold Bar Tango steps I had worked on with Miss Cummings in Palo Alto. I wanted to establish my bona fides early as an experienced teacher with this advanced student. I had arranged with Mrs. Huff the day before to meet in practice room number 2 upstairs at 3PM. I would spend the entire hour going over that one step.

At 3 PM, Mrs. Huff stood outside in the hallway with her dancing shoes in her hand. Somewhere around the age people retire from work, she had a small compact frame, stringy brown hair and a square face. Standing in the hallway with a disdainful look on her face, she said nothing. I invited her to sit down for a moment and tell me exactly what she hoped to get out of her dancing experience. She looked at me in a surprised manner as if I had asked her something I should have known or that was none of my business.

"I see from your folder, Mrs. Huff that Mr. King had you on International Styling in some of the steps," I noted.

"Yes, that's correct," Mrs. Huff answered.

"And how do you think you are doing?" I asked.

"I was doing fine," she responded, looking out the only window in the small room.

"What were you stressing in your program at the time? I asked." Standing up, Mrs. Huff said in a rather loud voice, "Look! I think it should note in my folder what I was working on -- in all the dances. Are we going to get started?"

With that outburst, I walked over to the small table and placed a 78 rpm record on the player and pressed the start button. I took Mrs. Huff's hand and led her to the center of the dance floor. Before we could get started, however, the door swung open and Stephens stuck his head into the room and asked. "Is everything all right in here?"

Mrs. Huff, somewhat surprised and looking at me said nothing.

"Everything's fine" I said.

"Are you sure," Stephens insisted.

I glanced up at the small register for the exhaust air duct located about a foot below the ceiling level.

"Well, I just wanted to make sure that everything was going all right in here," Stephens snapped as he left the room.

"Where were we?" I said, as I took Mrs. Huff's hand again.

Mrs. Huff didn't answer. Instead, moving slowly, she took my hand. Assuming the dance position l led her carefully through a series of the most basic Gold Bar Tango steps.

The record on the player reached the end of its grooves. The languid strains of La Cumparisita stopped and the needle scratched over the loudspeaker. I released my hold and Mrs. Huff walked slowly away, her eyes turned downward. She shook her head slowly from side to side.

"'I have prepared a new step for us to work on during our lesson today," I said, walking towards her looking over the top of a small bald spot on the back of her head.

She turned quickly saying, "Oh! What step is that?"

"Well, it's number twelve on your Gold Bar Program. It involves a heel turn, a series of four pivots and finishes with a media-corte."

"We had already done that step," she answered, "Just before Mr. King left."

"It's not marked off in your plan," I said. She did not respond for several seconds. When she did she annoyingly said, "Can't you understand? We didn't perfect the step. We worked on it, I said." She walked over and started to look out the window again. With her back to me she said, "We never marked off anything in the book until we perfected it."

"I see. Well, let's see where we stand on the step now," I said taking Mrs. Huff's hand and leading her into the center of the room.

Mrs. Huff, for whatever physiological reason, seemed to perspire profusely despite low ambient temperature and with little physical activity. This often made the back of her dress below her armpits feel moist. For that reason I would often place my hand lower on her back than ideal. This, accentuating the effect of her short but solid body, made it difficult for my long, slight frame to lead her at times.

When I pushed off to lead the step she did not follow at the "heel turn." As a result, my foot hit hers and we stumbled with my body almost falling over her.

"This is ridiculous," she exclaimed. "You don't even know that step! I don't think you know any of the Gold Bar steps," she said, again raising her voice. I looked up at the ceiling-air-register again.

"Mrs. Huff, I've danced that step hundreds of times."

"I never had any trouble doing it with Mr. King."

This time **I** walked away and looked out the window. Across the stree a man and a woman kissed directly in front of the Pizza Parlor. I turned and walked over to Mrs. Huff leaning against the mirror and grasped her by the arm.

"Look," I said. "I'm not Mr. King. Nor will I ever be Mr. King." She said nothing, but continued to look annoyingly at me. "I know he was an excellent dancer and had a lot of experience. I know he had a strong lead." For the first time, now, my voice began to rise. "I can't be him. So why don't we just forget it." I hesitated for several seconds again, but finally said what I really didn't want to: "If you want, I'll ask Mr. Fox to assign another instructor to teach you." (Actually, I knew we didn't have another Gold Bar–Certified Instructor in house at the time. She knew it also.).

Mrs. Huff didn't answer. We had begun to wear a path in the waxed wooden floor in the direction to and from the window.

After returning she faced me directly and placed her hand on my shoulder.

"Let's try it again," she said.

I had my first lesson with Mrs. Newbold on the same day. She suggested we just dance for the first lesson. "I feel a little stiff today," she said. "I can't concentrate when I feel this way."

I placed Mrs. Newbold in her mid-seventies at the time I knew her. If you were called upon to make a case for the benefits of ballroom dancing for older citizens, or to justify the programs of the Arthur Murray Dance Studios, you would probably cite her example as the centerpiece of your argument. If all students had the natural dancing ability, the style, the gracefulness -- and in particular, the personality of Mary Newbold, instructors should have paid Arthur Murray's to teach.

Because I knew she enjoyed the smooth dances, I chose the largest of the practice rooms upstairs to teach Mrs. Newbold. I selected 78 RPM Waltz, Fox Trot and Tango records from the cabinet and stacked them on the automatic record changer. Mrs. Newbold smiled as I took her hand and led her to one corner of the room.

For the next twenty or thirty moments the player rasped out the nostalgic strains of The Tennessee Waltz, Our Town, and La Puerta melodies. Using Mr. Fox's principle again, I led Mrs. Newbold through the most basic of the Gold and Gold Bar program steps.

Mrs. Newbold had all the qualities and dance habits of a good female dance partner: (1) she followed explicitly just a fraction of a micro-second behind her partner (she never "anticipated" or moved ahead of her partner even if she knew the step coming -- a fatal fault -- incurable in some women); (2) she provided a continuous, ever so slight, "resistance" going backwards (allowing the partners to stay together in all movements as one); (3) she pushed off with her trailing foot and took long strides backwards; (4) she maintained the "straight line" bodily posture as if a stake were driven through her from her head to her toe (never "ducking' down on an underarm turn). And most importantly, people enjoyed watching her dance because they knew she enjoyed every moment of it by the never failing smile on her face.

The studio had a low-toned bell that rang every hour. It always struck me as demeaning -- as if to marshal school children. It did, however, keep your scheduled hours on track. When the bell sounded, the last record on the stack had dropped -- an Argentine Tango. Mrs. Newbold looked up at me with a questionable expression. We continued to dance for another five minutes until the needle scraped.

Mrs. Newbold spoke very little. She merely smiled, thanked me for an enjoyable lesson and said that she would see me next week.

(I mused how much I should have paid Arthur Murray for teaching that hour?).

A new face showed up at the studio one Monday. Mr. Stephens introduced Mr. Reed to us all after the regular business meeting at 1PM. He had black curly hair, large jowls that parted wide when he smiled and virtually no neck. His frame -- over six and one-half feet in height -- had attended far too many functional dinners. Shaking his hand, it completely enveloped mine. He lumbered when he walked, his massive weight shifting from side to side.

I could never determine Mr. Reed's exact job description. His and Rodgers' purpose appeared to overlap, but seemed to come from different antecedents. He came in and stayed regular hours from 1 to 10 PM. He occupied himself mostly in the office looking over books, read a lot, wrote on a note pad -- an accountant, financial advisor, a public relations expert? He talked often to Rodgers and Stephens for long periods with the office door open. At all the parties he danced (leading very fundamental step patterns) with all the female students. He conversed with them incessantly -- at the parties, in the hallway, on the way into the studio, on the way out, at the coffee table -- wherever or whenever he made contact. He would even break in on a private lesson and ask questions that usually resulted in a conversation involving the student's interests and circumstances. He soon knew some of my student's personal situations more completely than I did.

"What if I leave work early -- at about nine? I can pick you up twenty minutes later. You should be home by about eleven." I held the pay phone in the hallway with one hand and my lesson clip-board in the other. 'The soft tones of "Awe, let's forget it this week," rasped through the speaker in the front base of the public pay phone. "We can go there next week, maybe. I don't feel all that great anyhow."

"Honey, that's the exact words you said last week. Do you realize that?"

"Really?"

"Yes!" I dropped the phone to my side. I picked it up and spoke more loudly. "Don't you even remember?"

"Like I said, I don't feel very well." I waited to hear more of an explanation. When none came I said merely, "OK. I'll call you next week."

My status with Sandy bothered me emotionally and my situation at school terrified me rationally: Ostensibly starting my junior year, I had to repeat two sophomore subjects, Thermodynamics and Statistics. In addition, my grade point average had fallen below the level required for upper division standing. Dr. Prione called me into his office again:

"I'm sorry, but you know we are trying to have the university accredited by the State of California and we must therefore keep our standards high. We cannot make any exceptions." He paused as if to make a point. "I would advise that you seriously consider, as I mentioned last year, that you downgrade to a technician's program."

"Thank you, sir," I said. I told him that I would think about it, but I really didn't mean it. I would have to find some way to have more time to spend on my studies. Or else I would drop out of school completely.

The winter months passed quickly. I continued to see Sandy, but only on special occasions. Only when she could find no excuse, it seemed. At first I thought it had all to do with my teaching of Joann Lavorne. Now, I suspected that "I'm the real problem."

With the coming of the spring season in San Jose, the rains stopped, the weather warmed and the state went in to its seven to nine month drought climate (between May and November it might rain one or two days -- maybe). The occupation of weather forecaster in the San Francisco Bay Area during summer months could challenge the simplest jobs on earth: "morning overcast, burning off around ten, producing clear skies, with temperatures of 75 to 80 degrees and winds up to 15 miles per hour." If you repeated that same forecast every day from May to November you wouldn't miss by very much very often.

With the coming of the summer season, the Studio began a concentrated "Lifetime Membership" drive. Lifetime Memberships became a pervasive tool for "up-front" cash flow enhancement in the early and mid sixties (particularly before the states and national government placed limits on its legal practice mid-way through the decade). Fitness centers, dating services, sport clubs, recreational programs and even bath houses would often require lifetime memberships as the only means to participate. The urgency for reform came from the tendency for the members to often outlive the company that provided the service.

To Arthur Murray's credit, unlike most other institutions of that day, they honored claims of one closed or bankrupt studio franchise at others. And at the date of this writing, the Arthur Murray business makes good Lifetime Memberships as far back as the sixties or before. They share the honor of this policy with very few other businesses.

One selling practice -- at least at this studio, however, seemed to transcend the pales that form the boundaries of human reason and logical thought processes -- "multiple Lifetime Memberships." How could you -- by whatever tour de force in salesmanship -- convince someone who had already bought a lifetime membership for a product or service to buy second or third or fourth lifetime memberships for the same product or service? Yet, this happened repeatedly at the Studio -- at times, with very little effort.

"$25,000 dollars?" Mrs. Jano smiled, took a long drag from a cigarette, blew a perfect circle diagonally upward across the table. She watched it drift into the air intake register close to the ceiling above Mr. Rodgers' head. "I could buy two single family homes in this valley for that amount of money."

Not missing a beat Rodgers said, "Mrs. Jano, the homes would do you no good if you were miserable inside the homes would they?"

"I'm not miserable, Mr. Rodgers, I'm doing fine. What makes you think that I'm so miserable? I have lots of friends; I have my retirement; I have my home; I have my health and I have enough to get by on." She paused again as if to catch her breath. "And, I intend to keep it that way." She put out the cigarette in the ash tray on the table, stood up and asked me if we could go find a room and start our lesson. Stephens looked over at Rodgers, but said nothing as they watched us leave the room. I did not teach Mrs. Jano any new steps that day. We sat part of the hour and talked. The rest of the time we just danced free style.

Before it came time for Rodgers to talk to Mrs. Wager about Lifetime Membership, I sat down with her in "private" (certainly not in one of the studio rooms but at the Pizza parlor across the street).

"I could do it I guess, but it would leave me little options for the future in terms of my finances. I would love to have the assurance of a lifetime of dancing, but I think I can do that by just buying separate programs. Then I have options. Do you understand what I am saying?"

"I got it."

When Mrs. Wager sat down with Rodgers and Stephens about Lifetime Membership she listened politely, smiled and said she would think about it and let them know. When Mr. Reed dropped by the small office to say hello, she responded graciously to his questions about her personal life and asked him reciprocally about his own. When he asked whether she would be joining their Lifetime Membership Club she merely said that she did not know. When they offered a 10 % reduction in the total price if she could let them know today, she insisted she would let them know later.

"Mr. Rodgers, I just had my 80th birthday six months ago. With whatever years I have left in my lifetime, I may not have enough time left to spend $25,000 if I live it on the French Riviera.

"Why not, Mrs. Livingston? You are healthy, energetic, and youthful in appearance. And dancing will help keep you that way for a long time," Stephens noted.

"I stay youthful by talking to you and Mr. Rodgers every year about some kind of new program."

Both men smiled, but did not say anything for several seconds. Finally, Rodgers finally leaned over the table and said in almost a whisper as if to make it sound more dramatic or sensational: "What if -- because of your special situation -- we gave you a 40% discount on the program?" Stephens opened his eyes wide and placing his hand on the top of Rodgers' red head and shook the young man.

Mrs. Livingston, however, seemingly unimpressed, merely placed her hand over her mouth and shook her head:

"No. I don't think so."

Rodgers and Stephens knew better than to waste time talking to Helen Fenner about a Lifetime Membership. She could hardly make the payments on her Silver Category Dance program. When they spoke to Joann Lavorne, however, they used all the darts hanging on the rack:

"Your youth makes this program particularly valuable to you, Miss Lavorne. You not only have many, many years to take advantage of it, but at your age you will learn so much more than an older person would," Rodgers spoke quickly. Miss Lavorne sat on the only chair located at the far corners of the small conference room

"But I already have the fully Amalgamated Program."

"Yes, of course. But this goes far beyond all your Programs. This covers you for a lifetime -- as new programs come into existence and new styles in dances emerge -- notably after your Amalgamated Program ends." Stephens stood up as he spoke and walked over to a blackboard in the small office and started writing.

"This is where we are now." He drew a long line on the board. "This is where the art of dancing will be 50 years from now." He made a small circle on the board. "This is you 50 years from now."

"Wow," the young lady exclaimed. "I can't even think of myself 50 years from now. I can hardly think of myself being 30 or 40 years old." She continued to stare at the board without saying anything. "I don't know if I would want to dance when I get to be that old."

"Trust me. You will," Rodgers suggested.

Again, she remained silent for several seconds. Rodgers and Stephens seemed reluctant to break the silence. Finally, the young lady spoke hesitantly without conviction in her voice:

"Well. . . Let me think about it. . . . That's a lot of money. . . ." She looked again at the board. "I'll have to think about that much money." She started to get up from her chair against the wall.

Before Rodgers or Stephens could reply, the door of the small room opened and Mr. Reed walked in. Looking around the room he went directly to Miss Lavorne. Grasping her hands with both his, he smiled and asked what was going on.

"Were trying to make Miss Lavorne a Lifetime Member, Mr. Reed," Stephens said.

With that remark, the handshake went to a hug. "Congratulations," he said, smiling. "We'll be honored to have you."

"It's a lot of money for me. I don't know if I can afford it."

The most overused line in the sales profession then, again, came out with a staccato, guttural sound from Reed: "Miss Lavorne, look at yourself. 'You can't afford not to take it. You're young, you're beautiful, and you're at a stage in your life where you will either go forward or go backwards socially, or in your career. You need dancing to move forward socially as well as physically. You only get one chance in life. Then it's gone."

Four men now, all standing in front of Miss Lavorne sitting on the chair in the corner said nothing but glared expectantly at the young lady. She started to rise.

Rodgers stood and walked over to the side of the room somewhat blocking her path towards the door.

"If you have the nerve and foresight to make a decision today, I can give you the whole membership for 15% off."

Miss Lavorne hesitated and stood in the corner of the room for several long seconds. She looked again at the board and then at Rodgers, Stephens and then myself. She spoke softly, "How much is 25,000 minus 15%?"

"Only, 21, 250," Rodgers replied.

"Wow, that's still a lot of money," she replied, now walking forward in Rodgers direction. Rodgers stuck his red head in her face and closed his one good eye and pretended to block her way again. Then, he smiled and slid aside as she continued to move forward.

"I better think about it. I'll let you know!"

During my lesson with Mrs. Newbold that week, Rodgers, again, stuck his head in the door and asked if he could see us downstairs in his office after our lesson. Later, at his office he shook our hands and led us down the hallway to the small conference rooms next to the main ballroom. This time we went into room number three.

Inside, the room did not have the usual large table with phone, wooden chairs and chalk board on the walls. Instead, it had only one comfortable lounge-type chair and an end table and phone. Mr. Rodgers invited Mrs. Newbold to sit in the only chair in the room. He and I stood on each side of the chair. He then removed a folder sitting on the end table and gave it to her. It read, Lifetime Membership, San Jose Studio. Mrs. Newbold, leaning back in her chair scanned the cover briefly. She then extended her arm and handed the folder back to Rodgers standing to her left side.

"I am already a Lifetime Member at this studio, Mr. Rodgers. Didn't anybody ever tell you that?"

"Oh, yes of course, Mrs. Newbold. I know that." Rodgers placed his hand on the elderly lady's shoulder. "We surely have that on record: you purchased a membership when Mr. Mock owned the studio back in 1955. And, we certainly have honored that and always will. We have continued your training through Gold Bar under that purchase."

Mrs. Newbold seemed relieved and leaned back in her chair looking up at Rodgers. Rodgers, however, continued to look at her with the same expression of interest. He placed his hand on his forehead as if to think of what to say next. Finally, instead of talking, he walked over to the only small blackboard in the room and started drawing separated circles on the board.

Before he could say anything further the phone on the end-table rang. "Excuse me," Rodgers said, and picked up the phone and listened. After several moments, he merely said "Yes, of course," and placed the phone back on the table.

"I'm sorry," he said. "Now, where were we? Oh, yes, Let me put it this way Mrs. Newbold: we have initiated many new programs here at the Studio in the last several years -- Amalgamations, International dancing, foreign competitions and new dances such as Salsa and

Merengue. We even have student/teacher trips and recreational excursions for students that at one time were not even considered part of a dance studio." He paused and studied Mrs. Newbold for a moment before continuing. "We have expanded or gone beyond the levels of what used to be called the Arthur Murray teaching system to include much, much more in the dancing experience."

He, again, stopped momentarily. "Let me give you an analogy: say for example that a person purchases a lifetime pass on a rail or bus line in a certain city. But suppose the rail or bus company expands the line to include other lines and other transportation facilities in the service. Certainly the original pass would not include the new services." Another pause. Mrs. Newbold said nothing. She continued to look intently at Rodgers. "What we would like to offer you now is the opportunity to participate in all the new services we have originated such as Amalgamation, trips, international dancing, foreign competitions and new dances that we as new owners have put in place. He then wrote each one of these items in the circles he had drawn on the black board and drew lines connecting them to each other. We can do all this for the one-time-only cost of $25,000. You would, by this purchase, not have another dancing cost for the rest of your lifetime." He placed the folder in his hand on the arm of the lounge chair. "This explains these additional programs in precise detail."

Mrs. Newbold appeared confused. She started to speak, but then placed her hand over her mouth instead. She looked directly at me with a vacant stare. I raised my hands at my sides. I must have had the same look on my face. Rodgers walked over to stand directly in front of her and asked, "Well, what do you think? Do you see yourself in all these programs, or not?"

The phone rang again and again Rodgers excused himself. This time a frown came over his face as he listened. He gave no reply but merely hung up the phone. He started to walk over to the lounge where Mrs. Newbold sat. Before he arrived there the door swung open and Stephens walked in.

With a broad smile and an open hand the young studio owner stormed into the room. Going directly to the lounge he grasped Mrs. Newbold's arm with one hand and shook her hand with the other. She could never act impolitely to anyone under any condition. She stood, smiled and gave him a quick hug. Stephens looked surprisingly at the chalk board and asked, "What goes on here?"

"I was just explaining to Mrs. Newbold the opportunity she has to become a new Lifetime Member."

"That's wonderful." Stephens, took one long stride towards Mrs. Newbold, now sitting again, and grasped both her hands. "We would love to have you! We call it our growing community." Mrs. Newbold, demure and somewhat quiet by nature, still continued to show no reaction and said nothing in response.

Stephens went to the blackboard and erased what Rodgers had written. In its place he wrote the words Medal Balls, Reno trip, Yearly Dance Party?

"Has Rodgers mentioned to you that all these events are included in your membership for free?" He pointed to the words, Medal Ball. "That the choreographing services of our Dance Director are provided free for all your medal balls or other competitions; that our annual weekend trips to Reno are included as well our yearly party at the Fairmont Hotel in San Francisco?"

Mrs. Newbold smiled, nodded her head slowly up and down, but still did not respond verbally.

"Wouldn't you enjoy the opportunity to go to some of these activities with Mrs. Newbold, Mr. Warner?"

"Of course."

The room became uncomfortably silent for several seconds as Stephens wiped clean the blackboard. When he finished he smiled and stood facing the older dance student. Before he could speak, again, the door swung open and the huge frame of Mr. Reed slammed quickly through the doorway. Seeing Mrs. Newbold, smiling, he strode quickly over to her and grasped her hand. "It's so good to see you again. How is your daughter, Stacey, doing with the phone company, Mrs. Newbold?"

"Oh! She loves it. The older women's face lit up for the first time. "She's now head of the financial department. Did I tell you?"

"No! That's great. She's only been there a few months, hasn't she? I'll bet you're proud."

"Absolutely."

"Mrs. Newbold is considering becoming one of our new Lifetime Members, Mr. Reed." Stephens now stood with Reed directly in front of Mrs. Newbold's chair against the wall.

"That's wonderful. You won't ever regret it. I know just how much you value your dancing and how much effort you put into it."

Rodgers now came over and stood alongside Stephens in line with Reed and myself now forming a line of four in front of Mrs. Newbold, still sitting with her hands on her lap in the corner of the room. He held the clipboard in his hand and a pen in the other.

"What do you think Mrs. Newbold? Do you have the ambition to take a shot at it," Rodgers asked.

Still, as her nature dictated, she did not respond verbally immediately. "I have to think about it," she finally said.

Rodgers now placed the clipboard on his chest. "Mary," he said, placing his hand on her arm (the first time I can ever remember him addressing a student by their first name), "I can help you make up your mind." He glanced questionably over at Stephens. "I can offer you a 20% discount on the whole program if you can make up your mind now -- a $5000 saving." "Mrs. Newbold, what are we missing? What is it that Mr. Rodgers has left out?"

"Nothing! I just have to have time to think about it."

Now, Rodgers dropped his hold on her arm, his tone of voice becoming louder and his speech quicker. "What is there to think about?"

"I'm just not sure I can afford it at this time."

Again, the classic one-liner of selling rhetoric: this time it came from Reed, his face now tense and his voice loud and booming -- accentuated by the confines of the small room: "Mrs. Newbold, you can't afford not to take this insane offer."

The four men, looming directly over the chair where Mrs. Newbold sat, parlayed a series of ongoing questions and answers. The noise in the room continued to swell. As their voices became louder, hers became progressively softer.

At the peak of the noise volume, Mrs. Newbold began to cough -- first just a mild, hardly audible rasp in her throat. She placed a handkerchief over her mouth. Then, she started to cough more violently. Placing both hands over her mouth she placed her head in her lap. With one convulsive burst she sprang to her feet almost hitting Rodgers in the face with her head. With both hands over her mouth, she murmured, "I'm so sorry." Her face in her hands she excused herself and ran out of the room, hoarsely whispering, "I'll have to talk to you later." She went directly into the Women's restroom down the long hallway in the direction of the front door. She slammed the door shut and stayed inside several moments. Later, she exited quickly and left the building.

I had often thought people seriously misinterpreted Mary Newbold's good nature, reticence and reserve as a lack of intelligence.

If management miscalculated Mary Newbold's sales resistance on the low side, they certainly miscalculated Dorothy Huff's on the high side. Called down to Robert's office, we again went directly into the small one-seated conference room by the large ballroom.

Again, Rodgers drew the circles on the board. Mrs. Huff leaned back in her chair and drew a nail file out of her purse. She filed as Rodgers pointed out how they honored her previous Lifetime Membership, what new programs they had instituted at the studio, and the analogy between the rail-line expansions and the studios "new" Lifetime Membership.

When he finished his presentation, he asked if she could see the comparison between the two.

Snapping up in her seat she responded jerkily "To what?"

"The rail line expansion and our new Lifetime Membership Program."

"Oh!" she paused while she moved to sit upright in the chair. "Sure, I see."

'Do you have any questions?"

Mrs. Huff did not answer but shook her head up and down. Rodgers then recited the new programs included in the Lifetime Membership and how it could affect her personal dancing. She now sat up straight in her chair. Before he finished she stopped him and asked, "How many other students at the studio are new Lifetime Members?"

"Only two right now," Rodgers answered.

"Will all the teachers know who the new Lifetime Members are?"

"Absolutely! And they will treat them for what they are -- the most committed members of our student body."

The phone never rang. And neither Stephens nor Reed entered the room. Rodgers didn't even have to offer the 20% discount. When he stepped forward and asked her what she thought, she, again, did not answer. With the continued bored expression on her face, she merely took the clipboard and pen out of his hand, signed the contract for a third Lifetime Membership and handed it back.

I have come to believe that Mary Newbold and Dorothy Huff -- despite some of the Machiavellian selling techniques employed in those days-- received dollar for dollar and penny for penny total value for the investments they made at the Studio. Though the antithesis of each other personality wise, they typified the most dominant genus of students at the Studio -- and perhaps most AM studios during that era -- senior women. As noted earlier (as diametrically opposed to post 20th century observations) I saw very few young students and even fewer young male students taking lessons in the sixties: mostly older women with, at the least, adequate finances.

The money these older women spent, however, I like to believe, they spent wisely: They enjoyed a badly needed communal relationship with the students and teachers in a "home away from home" like setting; it kept their minds active learning new step patterns; and, the health benefits of dancing -- particularly for elders -- has recently become universally acknowledged and proven by peer-reviewed scientific research:."

As alluded to earlier, in regards to a claim, the AARP web site clarifies the exact benefits of dancing to preserving health and mental acuity with age: Exercise increases the level of brain chemicals that encourage the nerve cells to grow. And dancing that requires you to remember dance steps and sequences boosts brain power by improving memory skills. . . ." It goes on to note that, "in a 2003 study published in the New England Journal of Medicine found that ballroom dancing at least twice a week made people less likely to develop dementia." Research also has shown that some people with Alzheimer's disease are able to recall forgotten memories when they dance to music they used to know.

Despite our partial breakup, Sandy continued to keep me informed on Mr. David's status when I would call her: It seemed they had not yet caught him subsequent to his break transferring to San Quentin. His brother had sold his house in Palo Alto and moved back to Oklahoma. I wondered why she took such a concern for his movements. I saw her only on special occasions when the two studios did something together. I wondered how long I could do even that.

My studies also continued to suffer badly. Now, even I wondered if Dr. Prione had it right -- I could never graduate as an engineer. I would not drop down to Engineering Technician in any case. I would rather change my major completely -- perhaps to Business Administration. Stay in the dance business? No! I didn't want to do that till fifty years of age. In the fall I failed another subject, Indeterminate Structures. Repeating it in the spring did not make it seem any easier. I evidently needed much more time available for my studies. I cut back my units to eight per semester. That helped enough so that I did not fail any subjects in the spring semester.

Daniel Gonzales continued to keep us all amused whether at parties or at night clubs. "When I come back in another life I want one of my lives to be as an Arthur Murray dancing student." Danny had a student, a woman who had taken lessons for over twenty years and had purchased a third Lifetime Membership. "I don't worry about it," Danny said, "She could afford to buy the Studio ten times over." He laughed, saying, "I'd like to have just one of her lifetimes."

The winter months brought the usual rain to the Bay Area. With Medal Balls coming up again in just two months, the teaching hours began to grow again. I had attended a six week summer session for three units. This allowed me to again take only eight units of classes in the fall semester. With this light load I managed to survive till midterms without any failing subjects. When I received my midterm grades I called Sandy to tell her the good news -- and to ask her to go out that weekend. A man answered the phone. The voice explained that he had answered in place of Sandy who was "busy in the kitchen." I asked him to try to disturb her. After a long pause, I heard him call her name. When I told her who it was, she said, "I'll call you back later."

END CHAPTER 6

Chapter 7

STUDENT EXCURSIONS

THE STUDIO HAD ONE OTHER formula for generating cash flow -- in addition to dance programs, introductory courses, competitions, amalgamations, lifetime memberships and medal balls: Excursions to resort areas accompanied by the teacher (the student paid his/her costs, the teacher's, and an included "management" fee to the studio).

Regretfully, I had to do all I could to prevent one of my students from purchasing one of the longer trips (if I missed a week or two of classes at school I might as well have dropped out for that semester). Sites for some of the longer excursions included Tahiti, the Hawaiian Islands, and the Philippines. I still feel the frustration over having had to miss those opportunities today. The Studio, however, did have many, shorter, long-weekend, excursions which I could handle. These included beautiful Lake Tahoe, Reno, the City of San Francisco and Las Vegas.

One Monday I came to work to find pictures of the main attractions of Lake Tahoe decking the walls of the studio in the main corridor. They had selected a weekend at the end of the month. Stephens greeted all the students with words of the coming trip to the scenic lake and gambling resort. Rodgers, of course, approached all my students. Of my students, Joann Lavorne and Edna Wager opted to go.

At I PM on Friday a rented bus stood on the curb in front of the studio as we all came to work. Many students had come early and grouped on the sidewalk at the bottom of the stairs, their handbags packed. The driver had already loaded suitcases into the side of the bus as the engine idled. Teachers and students arrived at random. The weak November mid-afternoon sun reddened faces of the talkative group. By 1:30 what seemed about thirty-five teachers, students, Rodgers and Secretary Carol Dixon had poured onto the bus. The driver, an old white-haired man with a handle-bar mustache, looked up and down the aisles counting with his lips. Finally, without saying anything to anyone he bounced into his seat. He slammed the floor-mounted gear shift forward. The motor started up like a present-day chain saw. The transmission whined in low gear and the blue, lumbering vehicle with rolled-up windows careened out into the center of Almaden Boulevard. Within moments we sped north on Highway 17 toward Sacramento. Inside the bus, ebullient students and teachers screamed to each other across the isles. Everybody seemed to want to talk at once.

Rodgers stood up and announced the itinerary for the weekend: We would check into the hotel on arrival. The group would meet for dinner at the hotel on Friday and Saturday nights at 7PM, lunch Saturday afternoon at noon and breakfast on Sunday morning at 9AM. In the evenings after dinner teachers and students would group in the fourth-floor lounge for dancing till midnight. On Saturday, after lunch, we would go as a group up the tram to the top of Heavenly Valley ski resort and view the entire lake area. All other times the students and teachers would be on their own.

By noon we had passed the outskirts of Sacramento along Highway 80. The back of the bus served as the staging area for food and refreshments. Carol Dixon and several of the female teachers distributed boxes to the students and teachers containing sandwiches and a fruit. On a rimmed table sat bottles of soft drinks and wine. After asking passengers their wishes the female teacher distributed drinks to the passengers. To fit the mood, most opted for small plastic cups of either red or white wine. By 2PM the noise level in the closed-window bus had intensified

As the female teachers passed through the aisles picking up empty boxes, the redoubtable Daniel Gonzales stood up and walked to the front. He proposed a toast to the weekend -- that all would have a great time; and, that all would come to know each other better by the end of our excursion. Then, he went immediately to the back of the bus. Several moments later he returned to the front. This time he had a new cup in his hand.

"How many singers do we have on the bus?"

Slowly, a few hands rose.

"How would you all like to try "Working on the Railroad?" Again, only a sparse number raised their hands. When Danny raised his hand and brought it down as he mouthed the first words, "I've been," however, a loud cacophonous sound rent though the isle of the large bus and reverberated against the walls. Soon, the notes became louder as the thump of the tires on the pavement seemed to accent the words of the old song. The highway changed into a two-way asphalt paved road as we approached the outskirts of the Lake Tahoe area.

Danny continued to lead the group in several other songs as the volume became increasingly greater and the clarity of the words increasingly less. Not long thereafter the singing degraded into only a lingering hum amidst loud laughing, talking and shouting by one passenger to another several seats away. In moments, Danny, feeling his way along the isle of the bus with one hand on each chair, again, retreated to his seat and sat down.

I sat next to Mrs. Wager. Joann Lavorne had no problem sitting at another seat several rows away (she would not sit alone for long). Another student, Mr. Englander, a middle-aged man with a large nose and a poorly-shaped toupee had his face in hers from the time we left San Jose to the time we arrived at the hotel. Even Mrs. Wager, the epitome of the demure and dignified woman, became unmistakably caught up in the spirit. We had our share of conversation..

Outside the bus, a light snow began to fall, turning green fields white and forcing branches to droop on the ubiquitous pine tree surrounded landscape. A sign read 6500 ft. elevation. As we sped along the single-lane road we approached an opening in the dense trees allowing the passengers to overlook the entire lake. Even in the snowfall the intensely clear blue color of the lake startled the passengers. The loud rasping sounds ceased as if an orchestra leader had slammed both arms downward. The sound of air rushing into lungs rent through the bus. Arguably, a scene of the most natural beauty on the planet appeared in panoramic view before their eyes (long before the '70s, '80s and '90s when developers would rape this natural paradise by converting it into an out of place, incongruous and environmentally-unfriendly gambling area -- which, as evidenced by areas like Reno and Las Vegas, can do well in a location completely void of natural beauty.

As the bus slammed through the dirt-and-rock-lined road to the main street of South Lake Tahoe, the passengers rolled from one side of the bus to the other yelling in unison at each sway. As we passed though Main Street, the passengers recited the names of each of the main casinos coming into view. Danny, standing at the front of the bus again began to clap as we passed one in particular. "Hey, that's my home there!" He continued to point as we passed the Hyatt on the driver's side of the bus. When we reached the South Shore Regency Hotel, the bus stopped and the driver exited the bus and summoned a bell hop standing at the curb. In moments, Rodgers requested we all follow. He walked up to the front desk and spoke to the woman behind the counter.

I had a room somewhere in the middle of the hotel. Mrs. Wager and Miss Lavorne had rooms on the top floor with views of the lake.

When we met for supper, each dressed in what suited them best: Mrs. Wager wore a blue blouse and white skirt that brought out her pure white hair and blue eyes. Miss Lavorne wore a black low-cut evening dress that brought out some of the men in the bar to take a second look. At supper we had two long tables in a separate room next to the main dining area. I sat next to Mrs. Wager and Miss Lavorne sat at one end of the table next to two of Miss Hudson's students. I had not really spoken to her much since the start of the excursion. She seemed satisfied, if not purposeful, in associating more with other male students than with me, which worked out great.

Dinner went on for several hours with the conversational noise level approaching that of the bus. At about 9PM, Rodgers stood and thanked all the students for making the trip possible. He invited all to join him in the main lounge for dancing.

The band in the lounge played a variety of dance rhythms that could not have suited the occasion better. Teachers -- as per AM protocol -- mixed with the students and did not dance exclusively with their own students. I tried to dance the smooth dances with Mrs. Wager. She looked elegant. I danced several Latin dances with Miss Lavorne.

Close to 12 PM, the dance floor started to thin out as some of the students retired for the night. A shade past midnight Mrs. Wager told me she felt tired from the long ride and would see me in the morning. I walked her to her room and gave her a hug at the doorway. She thanked me for a great evening. When I returned to the lounge floor, I saw Miss Lavorne sitting at the bar conversing with two men. One had on a uniform as if he were one of the staff. The other, a tall man with blond hair and broad shoulders, had an aquiline nose and wore a pin-striped suit. He looked "dapper."

Now, close to 1 AM, all the students and teachers had left the dance floor. Looking at Miss Lavorne talking with the two men, then at the almost empty dance floor, I turned, walked out through the lounge door into the hallway and waited for the down elevator. As I started to step into the elevator, however, a hand grasped my shoulder, A low, but somewhat slurred voice asked, "Hey, how about buying a girl a drink?" Miss Lavorne's eyes glared at me. They looked beautiful even with a red tinge.

I hesitated for a moment. People came by to use the elevator placing me in their way. Instead, I suggested that we go back in the lounge and dance (she didn't need another drink). At the lounge only two couples remained dancing. All of the Arthur Murray people had retired. The band played a slow Rumba which we caught about midway through the presentation.

For their next number they did a fast Argentine Tango, always my favorite dance. As noted previously, of all dances, in Tango, an experienced male partner can lead an inexperienced dancer through brute-physical dynamics -- and, force the style of the dance. Caught up in the music -- and, of course, perhaps -- the pulchritude of Miss Lavorne, I grasped her with the body-lead position and swept into the "stalking-the-prey-like" forward-lunge movements so characteristic of the Tango. I called up the best steps I knew -- and some I'm not sure I knew -- as we glided across the large lounge floor from one end to the other. Miss Lavorne responded well. As soon as we started dancing other couples sat down. The musical composition seemed to repeat itself over and over. The young student, however, did not appear the least tired and smiled continuously. The vocalist also smiled as we passed by her position at the front of the bandstand. When the composition finally ended, the couples who had sat down, and the others seated in the lounge chairs actually stood up and applauded. Miss Lavorne, somewhat shocked, waved a hand clumsily, giggled, and hid her face in my shoulder as we walked off the floor. Her eyes looked much clearer now. The band played the first measures of a slow Waltz and announced that they were through for the evening.

If I had purposed the dance to sober up Miss Lavorne, I had unmistakably scored a decisive victory. If I had purposed the dance as a self-aggrandizing ploy to impress the young lady, I had hit a home run in the bottom of the ninth inning of the seventh game in a World Series.

"One of the men I was talking to said that they have dancing in the Sky View Lounge on the top floor till 4 AM," Miss Lavorne noted, grasping my hand, as we returned to our seats.

Another long hesitation, I replied, "You talk to everybody, don't you?"

"I get around."

I did not answer directly; but, I also did not release her hand. I led her to the elevator in the hallway. Within moments we sat at a lounge chair by the window overlooking the complex of motels and one-story casinos that made up the nucleus of the south shore of Lake Tahoe's gambling district.

A waitress in a short red skirt came by and placed a napkin on our table.

"A vodka martini, please."

"Miss Lavorne, why don't you just have a soft drink."

"Just one! I'm OK. Trust me."

"One!"

The band resumed playing -- apparently after a short pause. The small floor soon filled with bodies coming from all directions in the lounge. The music, mostly slow, dreamy popular music of the sixties era, filled the lounge, sided on three sides by floor-to-ceiling bay-windows with a haze like atmosphere. The small rectangular space soon filled with couples. Unlike the setting at the lounge on the first floor, this crowded space provided no opportunity to dance any form of patterns. Couples stood together and moved minimally in swaying motions to the beat of the music or just stepped forward and backward ("belly-rubbing" music -- as the dance profession calls it).

The waitress came by and placed our drinks on the small table. I looked around the room. I saw nobody that I recognized -- surprised that none of the teachers or students had stayed up. Miss Lavorne took a small sip of her drink. Tiny mirrors on a revolving ball in the ceiling reflected a floodlight focused on it sending random flashes of light in all directions. Each pulse in our direction sparkled randomly off one of her clear blue eyes. The other eye, hid by a lock of jet black hair, peeked only when she thrust her head back. Even in the dim light of the lounge her chiseled features and cupid-bow mouth had men in the lounge casting furtive glances in our direction. She then placed her hand on my arm.

"Do you dance, Mr. Warner?" She said smiling

"I have tried at times," I replied.

"Well, why don't you try now?"

When we arrived on the small rectangular floor I tried to stay somewhat on the outside of the mass of moving bodies crammed together on the small dance floor. Unlike the formal dance position, I held Miss Lavorne in a loose grasp and merely swayed side to side with the music. She placed her forehead on my cheek. Instinctively, our position closed. A lock of her soft black hair covered my mouth and nose. Whatever perfume she had chosen, it suited her well -- as did the dress she wore. God had certainly placed all of her body parts in the correct location in the correct proportions. The silk of her dress rubbed against my waist and chest as we moved. My hand placed on the small of her back touched bare skin. Every part of her seemed soft and warm. I can remember feeling her pulse softly against my cheek. I could see out the side window to the parking lot below. Light snow had begun to fall and people ran from cars to the front entrance.

I don't remember how long we danced in that small cubicle. And I don't remember what she had said, if anything. I do remember that we did not sit down between songs for at least half an hour. After whatever length of time, however, the band stopped playing and announced that they would take a break and return in twenty minutes. We sat at our window table and sipped our drinks.

"So, what made you get into the dance business?" she asked, placing her hand over mine.

"Didn't have any other marketable skills, I guess. Needed a job. And, wanted to learn how to dance."

"Surely you knew how to dance when they hired you."

"Not really; they trained me."

"Perhaps I should become a teacher."

"Why not?" I looked straight across the small table at Miss Lavorne. "Tell me, why did you want to take dancing lessons?"

The young lady looked down at the table and spoke slowly and softly. "I don't know. I guess that I always want to do something that makes people notice me. I wanted to be an actress, but I don't think that I can act very well." She took a small sip of her drink. "My parents died in an auto crash when I was only a month old. I drifted from one orphanage to another until I was twelve. I always thought I had to compete. I always tried to outperform others at the institutions. I think I became very self-serving."

"I'm sorry," I responded.

"Oh, don't feel sorry. I now have good foster parents who take very good care of me." She smiled. "They also have lots of money."

"You certainly have the looks to be an actress. Are you sure you can't act?"

"Trust me. I've tried -- often."

The band started playing again. We returned to the floor for at least another hour. When they packed in their instruments for the final time we sat for a few moments looking out into the parking lot. Finally, I offered my hand and we walked across the top floor to her room. The halls, now vacant, still had a minimum of sound coming from parties going on in some of the rooms. When we reached her doorway, she placed the key in the door slowly, but spun around quickly, grasped the back of my head, kissed me full on the lips and held it several seconds. "Thank you," she said. "I really enjoyed this evening." She then slipped into the open doorway and stood for a moment.

I stood facing the doorway for an instant without moving. I placed my hand on the doorknob and looked quickly up and down the narrow hallway. I took a handkerchief out of my pocket and wiped any lipstick off my mouth. I started to enter the room, but instead, spun around and stood still. Later, listening to the varied cacophonous sounds from the ballroom, I walked slowly towards the elevator.

Getting only three or four hours sleep, at 9 AM I stumbled down to join the breakfast party in the main dining room in the basement. Mrs. Wager looked refreshed and wore a bright-red blouse and a pair of black slacks. The students and teachers talked loudly. Most ate several helpings from the buffet tables. By 11 AM the group marshaled in the front of the hotel to mount the bus for the tram to the top of Heavenly Valley Ski slopes. Miss Lavorne had not yet shown up. I checked over my shoulder every two or three moments.

On the bus, Rodgers mirrored the excitement of the students. He warned that no one should get too far away from the group. They were required to go up the tram and down again in line. If they missed the line, they would have no easy way to return. When the bus started warming its engine, Miss Lavorne had not arrived. I ran to the front and asked Rodgers if they could wait a while longer but he said that they had to make a time window at the tram. The bus therefore left without her.

On the bus Mrs. Wager seemed particularly in good spirits: "Did you sleep well last night, Mr. Warner?"

"Oh! Yes. Fine," I replied (for 4 hours, I thought).

"Didn't you think the band played excellent selections last night in the lounge?" she asked,

"Yes, perfect for dancing. I'm surprised. In this casino environment you might not expect that. I believe ballroom dancing is catching on all over the country. We go back to that that lounge for dancing again tonight."

"Yes. I'm looking forward to it."

The bus wound its way along the asphalt pine-covered roads bounding the lake from the South Shore to North Shore Lake Tahoe. The asphalt paving gave way to dirt as the bus left Highway 1 and bounced up the hill to the base of Heavenly Valley Ski Resort. Filing out of the bus, Rodgers ran ahead. He came back with tickets he gave to each of us. We walked only a short way to the tram boarding platform. Mrs. Wager and I and Mrs. Hudson and her two students entered the same tram.

Looking out the heavy glass windows we watched skiers in chairs spaced about twenty feet apart ascend the slope sporting red caps and brightly colored jackets. At the top the tram slammed to a stop and we exited and waited for the rest to arrive. The wind at the top of the mountain added to the cold effect. Some, including myself with only a light sweater had not dressed warmly enough. Soon, however, we sat in the sunny and warm confines of a glass-walled structure that served as a coffee shop and observation tower. When we sat at the tables by the window, we had a panoramic view of the entire lake.

Rodgers stood and narrated historical information about the lake area. He noted that this specific hill had been used for the winter sports in one of the Olympics. Mrs. Wager noted the steepness of the hill (Heavenly Valley does have some of the most challenging of all ski slopes, even today, for the most experienced skiers). The structure existed on tri levels: all the small round tables afforded a view of the slope downwards and the lake. Rodgers spoke to a woman behind the counter. Shortly, a young girl placed two coffee pots and a tray of assorted cookies and pastries on a table in the center of the room. The students and teachers formed a line, made their selection and returned to their tables. Fortunately, with the ski season not yet in full operation, we had the small coffee shop to ourselves. Cloistered in the warm glass-walled structure we enjoyed the benefits of the view and the warmth of the sun. We could watch the adventurous skiers traverse down the slopes in a winding path in order to brake their speed. Some chose to go straight down with increasing speed. Rodgers would point them out and we would all follow their path to the bottom. If everyone talked loudly on the bus, or on the tram, or at dinner, they talked louder here. Even Mrs. Wager shouted when talking to someone at the other side of the room.

On the way back to the hotel, we went completely around the lake in the long direction. This made the bus ride from Heavenly Valley to the South Shore Regency Hotel last about 11/2 hours. Through the pine trees, growing between the lake and the road, we could see the blueness of the virgin lake in its pristine form. When the bus skidded to a stop in front of the hotel, Rodgers reminded everyone about the itinerary for the evening: dinner at 7 followed by an evening of dancing in the lounge. I said my farewells to Mrs. Wager in the lobby and headed for my room. On the way I noticed Miss Lavorne seated on a sofa in the lounge talking to a young man. I turned my head and entered the elevator.

By supper time Miss Lavorne had not shown up. I searched the dining room throughout the meal. However, by the end of the dining period she still had not shown up. At about 8:30 Rodgers showed the pictures on a small screen and movie projector that he had taken that afternoon -- mostly of students and teachers getting off the tram.

After Rodgers' presentation, I excused myself and walked out into the lobby. I searched the lobby again unsuccessfully for Miss Lavorne. I called her room, but no one answered. I rejoined the group just as they left to go to the main lounge.

"Are you all right, Mr. Warner," Mrs. Wager asked as I joined her walking down the hallway. "You look disturbed."

"No! No! I'm fine." I replied. I took her hand and we followed the group down the long hallway into the lounge. We sat at a table with Mr. Gonzales and his student Mary Kurchinger. The band played a Cha-Cha rhythm and I rose and extended my hand to Mrs. Wager.

As per Arthur Murray policy, on excursions such as this, we mixed with all the other students. In particular, traded partners with all the students. This evening, however, I may have favored Mrs. Wager too much. Rodgers came over to me and placed his hand on my arm and said, "Hey, how about moving around a little." He then gave me a quizzical look. I nodded my head and asked one of Mr. Rodrigues' students to dance. After the dance, I slipped out of the room. I called Miss Lavornes' room. Again, no one answered.

Mrs. Wager and Mr. Gonzales enjoyed each others' company: she liked to laugh and he loved to make people laugh. Mrs. Wager, therefore, spent much of the evening laughing and the rest dancing. I felt pleased about that. The band played continuously for thirty minute periods. Then it would take a fifteen minute break during which time Mr. Gonzales would provide much of the entertainment.

By 11:45 the band had played three 30 minute sessions and taken a break. Mrs. Wager, having danced every dance of the three sessions, noted that her feet could not make it through another step. Most of the others agreed and began to leave the lounge. Rodgers left (making it official). I walked Mrs. Wager to the elevator. She gave me a hug, said she totally enjoyed the evening, told me to get some sleep -- that I didn't look like myself – and said that she would see me in the morning.

The hotel had a lounge or a waiting room close to the entrance where guests could group and talk. As I passed on the way from the elevator to my room on the far end of the first floor, I saw Miss Lavorne at the bar standing between two men. All had a glass in their hands. One of the men, a rather stocky man with a round face, had thick lips that seemed always open revealing white teeth. The other, a tall man with balding black hair, seemed to do most of the talking. All three had their backs to me   At the entrance to the lounge I saw the three still in the same positions. My leather heels, popular in those days, clicked on the waxed hardwood floors. When I reached the three I skidded to a stop. I stood clumsily somewhat off balance with my mouth half open. They stopped talking. Miss Lavorne exclaimed, "Mr. Warner!" I must have stood there for at least another second, frozen, saying nothing feeling foolish. Finally, I thrust my hand forward and grasped the young lady by the wrist and said, "Please, come with me." She, however, did not move. "Come on," I said. "I know a place where they dance till 4 AM every night of the week."

Miss Lavorne still made no response. Fat-lips placed his hand on my shoulder and said, "I think you had better let the young lady decide for herself what she wants to do."

"I think you had better take your hand off my shoulder."

"Oh! listen to the big man talk!" the young man exclaimed. "Look! I'm shaking with fear. What do you weigh, asshole, about 150 pounds?"

The man dropped his hand and stood back in a straddled-feet position, his nose thrust only a foot away from mine. Before anything could transpire, however, Miss Lavorne swept between, pushing us apart, screaming "Stop it, stop it! Both of you! Don't act like children!"

What happened next took me completely by surprise: She took a deep breath, glared at all three fixing everyone in place. She then grasped my hand, took a long step toward the door and said, "Let's go!" As we passed through the lounge exit I glanced back over my shoulder to see the thick-lipped one making an obscene parting gesture.

Outside the entrance I hailed a cab: "Hyatt at North Shore."

Miss Lavorne followed and sat at the far end of the back seat. She instantly and continuously had a smug "cat that ate the canary" look on her face. As the cab pulled out of the hotel entrance and hit the main street, light snowflakes hit the windshield but melted immediately. We said nothing for several moments as the cab careened through the hard concrete streets of South Shore Lake Tahoe. I looked straight ahead in our direction of travel. She nudged my arm to get my attention. She smiled as she spoke: "I've seen that look of anger you had on a man's face before."

"Oh! I'll bet you have!"

"'You shouldn't feel that way."

"Where have you been all day?" I asked, as the car made a sharp turn throwing me towards her in the back seat.

"Well, let me see. I slept late. I was invited out to dinner. And, I made some new friends."

"You didn't care about missing our dancing in the lounge?"

"'Our dancing. How do you call it 'our dancing?' You're always dancing with the others.'"

"That's my job. You know that."

"Well. I'm here now, aren't I?"

"Yes, you surely are."

The car skidded to a stop in the light snow at the curved front entry to the Hyatt. I paid the driver while inside the car. Miss Lavorne had only a light sweater on top of her evening dress. I placed one side of my sports jacket over her head and we ran to the front entrance. Inside, she took off the sweater, rolled it up and placed it in her purse. Her short evening dress had no back to it from the waist to the shoulders.

The Hyatt had more ornate decorations and interior furnishings than did our hotel. Miss Lavorne looked around as we passed through the lobby and entered the elevator. I had the constant feeling that all the men's eyes followed our every step. When we arrived at the lounge on the top floors the band had taken a break. We sat at a small unoccupied table right next to the dance floor. We ordered drinks and sat staring at each other.

"Miss Lavorne, . . ." I started to say. Before I could finish, however, she grasped my hand and placed her fist on my cheek. Thrusting her chin in my face she shouted in a sort of whisper, "If you call me Miss Lavorne one more time, I'm going to slap you harder than my friend Chuck was about to had I not jumped in and saved your skinny ass back at the hotel."

"Hey! This skinny ass can take care of itself."

"'Oh! So sorry. You are the 'big man.' OK Rocky, have it your way, but just say it once so I know you can actually say the word, 'Joanne.'"

"Joanne," I said softly as I reached across the table for her hand. The band had returned and started playing a slow and dreamy version of "Unchained Melody." Arriving at the center of the floor we soon became immersed in a sea of bodies almost touching on all sides. Even the shrill sound of the vocalist, her voice projecting from only foot above the crowd, became muffled with the sound of moving bodies. ". . .*all my love, my darling, I've hungered for your love.* . . ."

I placed my cheek against her forehead again and made only small swaying movements in time with the music. At times we moved with the natural sway of the crowd. It occurred to me that I had spent all these years to learn dance steps. I certainly did not need them here. Everything about her felt warm and soft. The lock of hair in my eyes partially blinded me. Her high cheek bones rested firmly against my lower jaw. Even her hair had the smell of her perfume. When the music changed, we stayed on the floor. She looked up at me. I placed my hands over her cheeks and kissed her. I could not seem to let go. She said nothing but emitted low-toned sounds without opening her mouth. Between kisses her cheeks lay so soft and warm against my chin. Hidden from the seated crowd we embraced for several seconds at a time repeatedly between dances, between musical phrases and between songs.

At breaks we sat at the table with hands locked across the table. She asked the questions. I spilled my guts like the bottom had fallen out of a rain-barrel. I told her everything I had done in my lifetime from the time I had reached puberty. She learned the street I grew up on, the high school I attended, my first date and the name of my dog. Within an hour she knew more about me and my aspirations, my politics, my quirks, my opinions, and my accomplishments than my mother did. The waitress came by and I suggested we have another round -- that she try the house-recommended double-Singapore sling.

Sometime in the early morning hours the band played the *"Tennessee Waltz"* and announced that they were through for the evening (or morning, or whatever).

We stayed at the Hyatt another half an hour or so not saying much but looking out the window and at each other.

Finally, the waitress came by and started cleaning tables. Joanne had some trouble rising, but we made our way out of the lounge, down the elevator to the lobby and out into the parking lot. I hailed a cab and soon we exited the cab in a light snowfall at the front of our hotel.

Inside the lobby we hesitated a moment to get our bearings. She reached into her purse and brought out the key to her room.

"Here, you better take these." She brushed back her long black hair out of her eyes. "I feel fine. But you had better take these and make sure we can get the key in the door so that we can get into the room." (In those days they still used keys, not sliding cards.) She placed the keys in my hand, placed her cheek on my chin and grasped on to my other arm.

"Got it," I said heading down the hallway. She leaned on me as we walked to the elevator. On the top floor the hallway appeared empty. We walked down to her room almost at the end of the row of doors.

At her doorway, I fumbled for the key in my hand before placing it in the door. Finally, as the door opened she took a step inside. About to follow, my eyes glanced at the stairway from the floor below at our end of the hallway. Only four or five doors away, Rodgers and a young woman I had never seen before stumbled up the stairs into the hallway. Both looked around. Not seeming to focus immediately, Rodgers straitened up and looked directly at me and said, "Warner?"

I didn't answer directly, but waved an acknowledgment. I stepped quickly back out of the doorway and reached forward and grasped the young ladies hand.

"Good night, Miss Lavorne," I said, closed the door slowly, turned and walked down the hall to the elevator. Rodgers continued to follow me with his eyes all the way to the point where I entered the elevator.

Getting out of the elevator, I ran to my room. I fumbled with the key and finally slammed the door open. Inside, I ran to the phone by my bed. I stopped, looked up at the ceiling trying to remember. I dialed the number. It rang several times but no one answered. I placed the phone back on the hook and walked to the other side of the room. I picked it up again and dialed the number. Before it rang, however, I put the phone back on the hook. I took off my clothes, looked at the clock showing 5:45 AM. I then walked into the bathroom and took a long hot shower. Instead of trying to go to sleep, I just got dressed and went to the cafeteria and drank coffee.

When the group met for breakfast at 8 AM, Miss Lavorne was absent. At 10 AM the bus sat at the curb of the front entrance with the engine idling. Rodgers took inventory of all the passengers. He went into the lobby and spoke to the lady at the desk. In moments, Miss Lavorne, her suitcase partially open, her hair uncombed, a wrinkled dress draped over her body, stumbled onto the bus. She spoke to no one, myself included. She went to the last row in the back of the bus, lay down lengthwise and went to sleep. She did not wake up for the six-hour trip to San Jose.

I sat next to Mrs. Wager. I drank several cups of coffee at every rest stop we made along the way, tried to keep talking, stood up at times and walked about the bus, pinched myself, and tried never to let my eyes close. But, despite all my attempts to stay awake, I dozed off at my seat several times, sometimes for as long as half an hour. Rodgers came by at one instance and shook my shoulder. He grimaced, but said nothing. Mrs. Wager slapped his hand and told him to let me sleep. Curiously, later, Rodgers, himself dozed off. I shook him, waking him, and smiled. He didn't smile back.

When we arrived in San Jose the bus emptied quickly. Mrs. Wager -- her usual self -- had nothing but good words to say about the times she had (despite my discourteous falling asleep on the bus). Post farewell greetings, teachers and students, all somewhat tired, dispersed in all directions.

I gave Miss Lavorne a quick hug as she left the bus and walked quickly to her car. I exited the bus after everyone else, including Rodgers, had passed, and walked slowly to my car parked on a side street next to the Studio.

Driving to my apartment, my mind immersed in the statistical improbability of Rodgers happening to come along just as we had almost entered Joanne's room the previous night (what -- one chance in 100,000?). It certainly affected our "activities" for the remainder of the evening. Most importantly, moreover, it may have affected what I (or we) did for the rest of our lives. This pertains to both of our lives

The older I become, the more I believe that it may have been one of the most fortuitous occurrences in my lifetime. Joanne, for all her beauty, brought with her considerable baggage: certainly, psychological problems it would unmistakably take more than one person to solve -- although that one person might unsuccessfully invest a lifetime trying. I enjoy **not** thinking about that entire weekend -- or of my behavior therein.

END CHAPTER 7

Chapter 8

CORONADO

ONE OTHER FORM OF EXPRESSION for students' dancing involved "open" competitions. Here, dancers from Arthur Murray's, Fred Astaire, or any other dance studio (or independent dancers) could compete at all levels of dancing. These events took place at officially selected sites, usually four or five-star hotels with large banquet/ballroom capabilities. The Coronado Hotel and Resort in San Diego, California, met all these qualifications. This year's event, as usual, would take place on a weekend starting with an introductory dinner on Friday night. Lower level dancers would compete in ascending order starting Saturday noon with the Gold Bar dancers completing the competitions on Saturday evening. Judges would announce results and distribute awards late Saturday evening.

Rodgers, of course, interviewed all of my students about going to Coronado. Joann Lavorne had promised her parents to accompany them on a 21-day cruise of the Mexican Riviera, so she declined. Only Mrs. Huff and to my greatest surprise Mrs. Livingston opted to compete in the event. I spoke to Mrs. Livingston in private.

"Yes, I have had considerable pain in my joints lately," she noted. I have slowed down a lot. My doctor thinks that I should do something to get me to move more." She smiled, "This certainly will. I just hope that it does not appear ridiculous at my age."

"You never look ridiculous Mrs. Livingston."

Mr. Fox had agreed to choreograph an entire routine for both Mrs. Livingston and Mrs. Huff.

For the month preceding the event I did see Sandy -- at times. Clearly, the ball park, the playing field and even the game we played had changed: not so much what she said or did, but more what she did not say or do. On the occasions I saw her (seems she had more relatives to visit than an Italian grandmother) our relationship grew farther apart: she stopped talking about the future: she talked about trivialities; she talked about the Studio -- never about us. When I would try to redirect the conversation towards us, she stubbornly resisted.

I know she saw other men. "Hey, man, I saw your girlfriend getting out of the side of a plumber-contractors truck this weekend in Redwood City," Daniel Sanchez said one Monday afternoon. "Did you know that was going on?"

"Not really," I said. "But I knew something was amiss."

"Well, if she were to marry him she'd certainly never have leaking faucets."

"Or be short of cash," I responded.

I could not reconcile with any certainty what irrevocable problem Sandy thought we had in our relationship: She mentioned Joanne Lavorne, but I believe she used that as a diversion -- a smoke screen -- both to her own thinking as well as to mine; more germane, I believe, she began to doubt my ambitions, my persistence and even my character. She had reasons to support this thesis. In all fairness to her, I had been in school for almost four years and had only finished less than two years of my studies. Did she think I was lazy, poorly disciplined or just stupid? Did she become convinced that I would never finish school and spend my life as an Arthur Murray dance teacher? A great profession for a young, single man, but not for the family man she had envisioned for her husband. Whatever the case, nothing I said seemed to make much difference in our relationship.

I met my students at the airport in San Jose. Sitting with Mrs. Livingston, looking past her out the window, the combination prop-jet engines vibrated the long wings of the aluminum skinned airplane. We moved slowly away from the loading area onto the asphalt runway.

"You know, Mrs. Livingston, I always feel queasy flying commercial airlines."

"Oh! You will enjoy it, it's nothing," she replied, now looking out the window herself. "The only time I feel at all uneasy is on take off and on landing. If something were to go wrong, that's when it would occur, I believe."

"I'm sure you're right."

When we landed at the San Diego Airport, the plane bumped rather hard against the asphalt runway. I glanced over at my elderly student who looked unabashed. She smiled as the props reversed; we thrust forward in our seats. The plane shook somewhat but reduced to taxi-like speed.

The mild San Diego climate greeted the students and teachers as they exited the plane. We grouped and entered a bus waiting at the curb. The warm sun radiated in through the bus window as we approached the bay. Soon the profile of the giant multi-structured red-and-white-colored Coronado Resort complex thrust upward into our sight ripping apart the contour of smoothly flowing, sandy beach along the coastline. Comprised of a generous parcel of California's southern-most coast (purchased over a half-century ago by visionary founders at a time when this real estate sold at almost immeasurable fractions of today's values), its pillar-enclosed ballroom projects over pure-white sandy beaches. At night, the moon, reflecting off the tops of white capped waves, lasers through glass walls onto the ceilings and the well polished floors giving the rooms a natural sparkle during events. Only the occasional thunder of a large wave would break the pulsing sound of tiny wavelets striking the sandy beach line like the sound of breaking wine glasses. Located amidst one of the most perfect weather systems on the planet, if you had to make one unchangeable choice for a resort, you might choose this one.

When the bus stopped at the curved entry, the students scrambled to identify their luggage. Inside the giant registration hall, Rodgers assigned us rooms. I would share a room with Mr. Saunders, a beginning teacher who had been with the studio only six months. Saunders stood over six feet tall. His blond hair always seemed to fall in an unkempt -- but, perhaps, dashing -- fashion over a clear, blue right eye, accenting his wide smile and square jaw line. He seemed to lurch when he moved as if not able to completely control his long, rather loosely-jointed frame. Daniel Sanchez and Mr. Richards were assigned the room next to us.

Before dinner the four of us walked down to the ballroom. The loudspeaker played a smooth, but fast, fox trot rhythm. Already, several couples swashed with long flowing strides across the huge ballroom floor. Clearly dancing with "international" styling the partners stood erect with strained, accented posture, heads tilted back. The women strained but kept that smile fixed on their faces directed towards the ceiling. Moving so effortlessly and covering so much space with each stride, they traversed a full cycle around the outer perimeter of the ballroom in less than a minute. Certainly, they would compete at the Gold Bar Level. We all stood several moments watching. Danny placed his hands on his hips.

"They're not student/teacher," he noted.

"No. They're too good for that," Richards remarked.

"We need to get our students out here and run through their routines," Danny continued.

"I ran through ours this morning at the studio," I remarked. "With both students before we left for the airport."

"So did we," Danny snapped. "But it's not as good as on the actual dance floor. You know that."

"You're right. But it's too late to mobilize our students now before dinner. They'll move tables onto the floor for dinner soon and be there all night. I think we should try to get them down here early tomorrow morning before the competition starts at noon," I said.

"That should work," Danny replied.

Over the next several hours, crews moved dining tables into the ballroom to cover the entire spectator and dance area. Dinner started at six, but nobody sat for at least thirty minutes. As arranged by the studio, I straddled my two students. Mr. Fox sat at Mrs. Huff's left. She spoke seldom to me. If she could not attract Fox's attention, she spoke to one of the other teachers. In public she seemed to have a hierarchy with whom she would select to talk. Certainly, I did not sit high on that list. Nor did students. Obviously, Fox or most other teachers did.

Following the meal, Rodgers reviewed the particulars of the next day's events. By 8 PM the level of wine in the bottles at the tables had decreased considerably. The noise level in the room, inversely, had increased to where people shouted across the tables. Soon thereafter, Rodgers stood and started to leave the table. He noted that he would see them here at breakfast in the morning. He urged everyone to retire early. Dorothy Huff stood talking to Fox. Mrs. Livingston seemed glad to take Mr. Rodgers suggestion to heart. She grasped my hand and said she would see me in the morning. As she turned to leave, however, I grasped her hand and with my other hand stopped Mrs. Huff as she started to walk away.

"Could I see you both here at 7 AM, before breakfast, to go over our routine in the ballroom?" I asked.

"Again? Mrs. Huff asked. "We did that today."

"We want to get the feel of the arrangement on this floor."

"You worry too much," Mrs. Huff said, starting to walk away. "I have to make up my hair at that time in the morning."

To my surprise, Mrs. Livingston's long arm reached across my body and grasped Mrs. Huff's sleeve just below the armpit. "Listen," she said. "Mr. Warner's right. We need to go over the dance on **this** floor." She let go of the sleeve and looked directly at the startled Mrs. Huff. "You'll be glad you did."

Mrs. Huff didn't say anything. She merely straightened the sleeve on her blouse, looked at me and then down at the floor. She then walked slowly away. I smiled at Mrs. Livingston as she picked up the hem of her long dress and walked slowly toward the elevator at the end of the hall.

When I returned to the group, Saunders had joined Richards and Gonzales.

Without direction or any definable leadership we drifted out of the main ballroom into the hotel entrance and into the street. The unseasonably warm ocean breezes soothed our anxieties and refreshed our spirits. We walked out the cobblestone curved front entry onto the coastal freeway. We stopped several times to look out at the endless field of whitecaps stretching outward cold and dark as far as we could see. The moon, now only about one forth up into its equinox reflected toward us in a straight line.

As we looked out to sea, an old black late-forties-model-Ford station wagon pulled up behind us and parked at the curb. It had no ownership or company identification. It merely had the word "Taxi" brush-painted in white on the side of its front door.

"Hey, Padre's, where you go," the driver called out.

"Nowhere," I exclaimed. "We're just looking at the ocean."

"Why dun't you luke at the city," A round-faced driver wearing a straw hat called out. "Have you seen city? It's a beautiful city."

"No. Thanks. We have to go in soon."

"Hey, wait a minute," Saunders exclaimed. "We aren't ninety years old. Let's go for it. We may never have a chance to see San Diego again. It's still only 8:30."

No one moved or commented for several seconds. Finally, Danny opened the back door of the old car and began to get in. "I'm with you, Craig. Come on, guys, we only live once. Let's just see what the town looks like."

Reluctantly, I said nothing and followed the other three into the cab. In moments we sped along the coastline away from the lights of the hotel complex on the beach into a field of darkness broken only by pulsing street lights toward a much brighter and much deeper field of lighting.

"This city limits," the driver exclaimed about ten minutes later.

"This, capitol building!" the driver looked out the side of the cab in all directions.

After several more stops at public buildings, he stopped and leaned over the front seat to face those in the back, "You don't want to see this, do you?" he called out. "Boring, no?"

No one responded to the driver's question. With no response to his remark -- either positive or negative -- the driver made a sharp right-hand turn and sped down a one-way street. We left an area of tall, concrete, well-lighted buildings with shops on the first floor. The buildings changed to red-brick construction with broken windows and no lighting. In spots, only foundations remained. Homes spaced between the building with front yards filled with old tires, beer cans and empty bottles. Soon, the width of the streets narrowed, the houses became smaller and ran together with a common wall between them and only a porch and stairs to the sidewalk. At every street corner, a bar and a grocery store sat on opposite corners at the intersection. He sped through at least twenty intersections. Finally, he approached one and stopped at the curb next to a bar with the entire front walls painted gold. The head of a gold-colored dragon protruded incongruously from the wall above the double-door front entrance.

"Hey! Why dun you try this?" The driver snaked his head past me in the front seat to talk to the others. "They have real good music here. And lotsa nice people -- girls -- very friendly."

"'I don't know." Richards remarked. "How do we get back to the hotel?"

"I come back in an hour. You want to go back, we go back. Or, I take you back later."

"Come on, just an hour," Saunders said. "What the heck. It's still early."

`No one, except Saunders, seemed to have any firm conviction, so we followed him and then one another out of the cab.

Past the second door the loud voices and smoke filled atmosphere hit us simultaneously. As the waitress led us to a round table, the band started playing a Dixieland jazz number. The blaring sounds of the band did not substitute for the crowd noise; it only added. Shouting our orders to the waitress, we appeared to attract the attention of the crowd in the small rectangular bar. The position of our table, adjacent a "postage stamp" dance floor placed us directly in front of several guests seated in a long bench directly behind us.

Saunders always attracted attention -- particularly from the opposite sex. As we passed the bar to our seats he must have made some form of eye contact with a woman seated at the bar. After we had sat only a moment or two, she called to him. He became engaged in a conversation with her directly behind us. In less than an additional moment, he stood and took a step towards the bar. When he returned, she followed and sat at an empty chair next to him.

Marie's long black hair, banded at the back of her head, fell down to her shoulders giving her hawk-like-nose profile an aggressive forward-looking thrust. She appeared considerably older than Saunders. That didn't bother him. After introductions, she noted that she, too, had flamenco-danced as a child in Mexico. We shared our experiences. She and Saunders joined the tightly-grouped mass of bodies swaying to the Latin rhythms on the tiny dance floor. Soon their bodies became immersed in the mass of swaying forms. Only Saunders' straggly blond hair appeared at times bobbing above the pack.

When the band finished one of its popular belly-rubbing-like compositions, Saunders' head pierced its way through the crowded dancers waiting on the dance floor and grasped the arm of the man standing in front of the four-piece ensemble. Saunders spoke in his ear. The man shook his head somewhat. Saunders spoke again. The man looked back at his crew. He spoke in Spanish. The man at the piano nodded his head. Now the man up front nodded his head. Saunders walked back into the crowd of dancers. In moments the band started playing a very bad but loud rendition of La Cumparisita, a classical and very definite Tango rhythm.

If someone had dropped a bag of hissing rattlesnakes into the middle of the closely packed group of dancers, it would not have cleared the floor more quickly. Our dashing hero now stood in the middle of the floor with only his long-haired, short-skirted partner by his side.

What Saunders lacked in experience or style, he made up for with movement and enthusiasm. Parts of his long, gangling body seemed to act independent of each other and appeared disconnected. His movements thereby jerked somewhat, but had a dramatic flair. All of this did not faze Marie, glued to his side, appearing intense but unmistakably proud as she strove to follow his lead. When the music stopped, Saunders and his partner stood in the middle of the floor laughing in a cheek to cheek embrace. The band resumed with its previous genre of music and once more the dance floor filled.

As promised, our driver appeared in about an hour.

"You ready to leaf -- or no," he asked.

As a group we all nodded. Richards walked onto the dance floor and spoke to Saunders. In a moment he returned without the young teacher.

"He wants to stay a while longer. Says he's having a ball. 'Don't worry about me, I'll take a cab home when I get through,' he says."

"I don't like this," Richards said. "He needs to get back. You know what Rodgers said."

"Hey! What are we going to do? We can't make him go back," Danny said. "He's a big boy now. He certainly can take care of himself."

"I guess." Richards replied.

When we left we all waved at Saunders who now danced with his head straddling the top of Marie's head. He paused only long enough to wave with one hand.

I found my way into bed somewhere between 11 and 12 PM. I looked over at the empty bed next to mine. The wind off the ocean blew in though the half-open window next to my bed. The sea breeze had a comforting effect on the thoughts going through my mind about Huff's, Livingston's and my own performance tomorrow -- as well as for Saunders. When would he come back?

I woke sometime around two AM to go to the bathroom. Saunders had not yet returned. When the alarm went off at six, I quickly scanned the room. His bed had not been touched. I didn't even know the name of the bar we had visited the night before or how to get to it. I called Richards and asked him if he knew. He didn't. He also had no other suggestions.

I showered, dressed quickly and called to Mrs. Huff's room. I had to go over the routine with her -- whether she wanted to or not.

"I can't make it by eight. I have not even started getting dressed. We will have to eat breakfast late." Mrs. Huff's voice sounded exceptionally shrill over the hotel phone. "If you had prepared our routine more, this would not be necessary. I have never had to do this before."

At eight, I met with Mrs. Livingston. Fortunately, we were able to play our music selection over the public address system. We went through our entire routine three full times. Other contestants had not arisen yet, I thought. "That really helped me feel better," Mrs. Livingston noted. "Thank you so much for taking the time to do this. I really appreciate it."

`When Mrs. Huff met me in the ballroom at 9:15, at least six other pairs traversed over the floor to whatever music played over the speaker system. We therefore had to practice our Fox Trot routine to Tango music. Mr. Fox had choreographed a rather difficult heel-turn-spin-into a Media Corte followed by a set of pivot turns that we never could perfect. We rehearsed it several times without success. "I never had any trouble doing heel turns with Mr. King," she had to say.

"Please, don't start that again," I said. "Let's go over it one more time."

As we danced, Mr. Fox appeared in the ballroom and came over to the spot where we finished our routine.

"That doesn't look bad." He said. "But let me show you that heel-turn combination one more time. In his arms, Mrs. Huff did it perfectly. I could see it -- and certainly she knew it. To her credit, she said nothing. The manner in which she looked at me, however, required no spoken words. Mr. Fox left. She merely said she'd see me this evening.

As I walked out of the ballroom, Rodgers met me at the doorway. "Where's Saunders," he asked.

"I don't know," I answered.

"What do you mean you don't know?" Now he shook my arm. "He's your roommate. You don't know where he is?"

I immediately pulled my arm from his grasp and stared at him. "I'm not his mother. What am I supposed to be, his guardian angel?"

Rodgers' countenance suddenly changed. He placed his hand on my shoulder and almost seemed cordial. He spoke in low tones: "We can't afford to refund the money to Mrs. Cunningham for not doing her routine at this competition." He pointed down the stairway to the hotel basement. He led the way and I followed. "Look, she's just a beginner student, so they have a very simple routine worked out." When we arrived at the bottom of the stairs, he led me into a small room with no windows. Mrs. Cunningham stood in one corner of the room practicing a series of dance steps.

"Mrs. Cunningham, you know Mr. Warner. He's an advanced teacher. If you show him the steps you were to do with Mr. Saunders, he can dance the routine with you tonight."

"Do you think you can really do that, Mr. Warner?"

"Piece of cake, Mrs. Cunningham." I walked over to where she stood and took her in a dance position. "Shall we try?"

Rodgers had it right. Mrs. Cunningham knew the steps as if she had designed them herself -- Tango, straight from the beginners Bronze program. And, I had done them all ad nauseum many years prior. Consequently, after only about a half hour of practice I had gone through all the steps of the routine with her. Now, if I could only remember the sequence for the performance.

"We had better come down here again after lunch and go over it again," I told Mrs. Cunningham. "I'll see you at lunch and set an exact time."

Because my two students competed in the Gold (Huff) and Gold Bar (Livingston) categories, I had free time in the afternoon (Gold and Gold Bar competition did not start until 4 PM. Mrs. Cunningham's routine would take place at 1:30 PM).

I returned to my room about 11:30 to take a quick nap before lunch. When I entered the room, I heard what I had hoped to hear all last night. Saunders lay draped over his bed in his dress clothes snoring. I ran over to his bed and shook him. One eye opened and glared at me. I ran over to the sink and came back with a glass of water. Pouring it into his face, he shook his head placed his hands on the side of his face and started to scream, "Get me a bowl. Please, hurry." I raced over to the counter and reached down below the sink and found an old wash pan. Racing back I arrived just as he emptied his stomach into the bowl.

I walked quickly back into the small bathroom, slammed the door shut and listened. Hearing footsteps I walked out the door as Saunders walked in and emptied the bowl in the toilet. He then stumbled out the door and fell head down on the bed. He lay still. I stayed by the bathroom door. After several moments he raised his head and just stared at me.

"What time is it," he mumbled.

"It's about noon."

"Oh my God," he said. "Look on the program and see what time I go on with Mrs. Cunningham."

"I don't have to look. It's at 1:30."

"Oh! Thank God," he screamed. "I thought I was late."

"You are late. You can't dance like this."

"Like what?"

"You're drunk, Wayne. And, you haven't had any sleep."

"I just slept."

"Oh, sure, how much?"

"I don't know. Since I got back."

"What? One hour?"

Saunders got up from the bed and stretched. He then placing one foot carefully in front of the other and walked slowly to the bathroom. "Look! Do me a favor. Just order me a coffee dispenser. I'll take care of the rest."

If the parts of Saunder's long body appeared to act independent of each other in a floppy fashion when sober, he now looked like a walking string of beads. Though divagating and yawing off course several times, somehow, he managed to careen his way into the shower and turn on the water. Letting out a scream, he slammed against the four sides of the wall before obtaining the temperature he wanted. In less than five minutes, however, he ran through the bathroom door and searched naked through the trunk located next to his bed for underclothes.

Just as Saunders adjusted his vest in the bathroom mirror, the bellman wheeled in a trolley with a pot of coffee and pastries. Two cups, a bagel and a trip to the bathroom and he stood in the doorway ready to go.

I should try to stop him, I thought. But, I had seen that look in the young man's eyes before. Instead, I didn't mention that I had rehearsed with Mrs. Cunningham. I merely gave him one of my Lifesaver Mints and followed him to the ballroom.

Now about 1:10, Mrs. Cunningham, standing next to Mr. Rodgers, waited in the small dressing room next to the main dance floor. Seeing me first, she called out, saying she had expected me to phone her. Seeing Saunders lope in behind me, she rolled her eyes, placed her hand over her mouth but said nothing.

Saunders, his usual personable, gregarious self, smiled and took Mrs. Cunningham's hand and said, "Are you ready to go?"

"Yes, I am," she said. She leaned back and looked at him from the side. "Are you?"

"Of course," Saunders replied.

His movements, however, appeared somewhat unsteady over the next ten moments as he lopped through several of the steps in the semi-darkness of the small waiting room.

When they walked out into the main ballroom, the crowd had not yet completely gathered. Empty chairs pock-marked the spectators' tables forming the periphery around the oval-shaped dance area. They stared tentatively for several seconds with Saunders appearing somewhat unsteady. When the spotlight went on and the music started, however, like the flipping of a double-throw double-contact electrical breaker, the young-man's body seemed to inflate, to energize cross-flowing circuits in all directions at the same time. His broad smile never leaving his face, his blond hair lofting from side to side across his upper forehead, he sprung off with Mrs. Cunningham glued to his hip. Making up for the lack of posture and rigidity with animation, flair and movement, he loped through every one of the selected Tango steps without a single miscue. Mrs. Cunningham bowed, blushed and returned to the dressing room with a broad smile on her face unmistakably pleased. (Who ever said that life was fair?)

Mrs. Livingston had her Gold Bar Quickstep competition set for 4:45 PM and Mrs. Huff set for 5: 30. By 2 PM my elder dance partner had called my room twice and sent the bell boy in search of me. At 4 PM I called her and told her I would meet her in ten minutes. She worried too much! Mrs. Huff, not enough!

Walking from the small dressing room to the center of the dance floor I could feel Mrs. Livingston's hands quiver. I wondered how she had the nerve to put herself through this type of stress at her age. In addition, doing a quickstep routine only added to the physical commitment required. She always seemed to feel it necessary to challenge or push the envelope of her physical abilities to the limit. I admired her for that.

When we took a dance position, however, she felt as rigid as a stone fence. The lines on her long face looked so much deeper now. She tried to smile, but facial movement only deepened the wrinkles along her chin. I encouraged her to relax. "It's only a dance. It's for fun. And, you know all the steps backward and forward."

Mrs. Livingston's heel must have turned under her foot on the first long step forward. She stumbled backward. Fortunately, we did not fall. It did, however, create an obvious flaw and marked discontinuity in the routine. And, we were forced, visibly, to abort the step. Subsequently, her body became even less flexible. Admirably, she never quit. We traversed through the remaining steps of the routine -- though sometimes somewhat tentatively with less than elegant styling. When we finished, she seemed, if nothing else, relieved. I did also.

I never felt nervous when I danced with Mrs. Huff. Perhaps a defensive antipathy substitutes for nervousness in the human persona. I met her in the practice room prior to our dance. She wore a red dress with a black skirt that touched the floor. I told her that she looked very nice. She made no response. She merely looked at me disdainfully and took my hand in the dance position. We practiced the first three patterns of our routine. We performed the heel-turn pivot combination once with success but two times without. Again, I heard it regarding Mr. King. We walked over to the side of the room and waited saying nothing. Marching out to the floor I felt neither anxiety nor pride, mostly resentment. I just wanted it over. Perhaps anger secretes a chemical substance in the brain that fuses the unconnected strands of tenacity. Whatever the physiology, I felt capable, determined.

Though Mrs. Huff carried far too many pounds on her short frame, she did have excellent posture. From the time we jumped off into the smooth steps of the Fox Trot patterns she held her smile-fixed face girded back pointing at the ceiling.

Since she had such a "squat" physique I had always considered us as somewhat of a mismatch because of my long legs. For this reason, I may have always shortened my steps to account for her size (a technical fallacy: shorter women can take very long steps by the "pushing off" technique). Now, however, the anger I felt may have overcome this consideration. Whatever the reason, I thrust forward with as long a stride as I could in each of the steps. Mrs. Huff's eyes opened wide and glared at me. Automatically, in response, however, she pushed off and took much longer steps herself. As a result, we traversed the perimeter of the floor much farther than we ever had in our practice sessions -- or in any of our previous dancing together. And, our dancing felt more animated and moving. It even made the routine pass more quickly.

Performing our heel-turn-pivot sequence -- because of our longer strides and greater speed -- we spun into and through it much more quickly. Perhaps because we had less time to anticipate or worry about it, we did it perfectly. Encouraged by that, we finished the remainder of the dance better than I could have hoped for. The smile on Mrs. Huff's face lasted much longer than it took us to bow and walk back to the dressing room. There, I told her I thought she did well. She did not reply. But when I shook her hand and left the room, I thought that she gave my hand a slight squeeze.

The Awards Dinner always became the "piece de resistance" of the event. Also, with the performances over, the students and teachers could enjoy their meal with greater relaxation. Only the decisions of the judges remained. Student/teacher partners did not win the majority of these type competitions. Individual dancing partners either from smaller studios or independent professional dancers had an edge because of their close relationship with each other over a longer time frame. For example, Mrs. Livingston or Mrs. Huff had never placed in the top three previously.

Mrs. Livingston did not appear disturbed by her performance. Certainly she could have done better. "I accomplished what I wanted," she said, placing her hand on my arm as we sat down for dinner. "I feel strong, relaxed and energetic." Nothing she said could have made me feel better. I believe she knew that.

Mrs. Huff chose to sit with us and sat quietly across the table. At dinner she spoke to all, including myself, graciously complimenting those who performed. By the time dinner ended the group at the table had melded into a relationship of close companionship and understanding.

The hotel had placed a platform about twelve foot square and two feet high in the geometrical center of the oval-shaped ballroom. This allowed all guests a direct view of the platform. A table sat on one end with rows of small trophies graduating in size from front to rear. Here, contestants would mount the stage on one side, receive their award, have their picture taken and exit on the other.

In beginners Bronze Tango category -- to their genuine surprise -- Cunningham and Saunders won a second place finish. In the gold Waltz category Hudson and her student Mr. Klein won a third place trophy.

When the announcements for the Gold and Gold Bar categories began, we did not pay close attention. Even Mrs. Huff talked freely with others at the table as the proceedings progressed. When she heard her name called for a third place award in the Fox Trot category she sincerely gasped and placed her hand over her mouth. Genuinely surprised she stood and waved and walked quickly to the awards table. Returning to the table after accepting the trophy -- for the first time I could remember -- she blushed and sat down quietly and solemnly. Her countenance had completely lost its hauteur, its bluster.

The noise level in the section occupied by the teachers and students far exceeded other areas of the plane on the flight back to San Jose. Rodgers walked up and down the aisles talking to each and every student. Even Miss Hudson, usually so reserved, traversed the section speaking to students and teachers at random. When we landed in San Jose, the students seemed almost reluctant to get off the plane. Mrs. Livingston's husband met the plane and had already picked up her baggage when she arrived at the baggage terminal. She gave me a hug and ran into a cab. Mrs. Huff had her baggage already on a cart. She stopped long enough to face me standing next to the exit door. I walked over to where she stood. She certainly didn't hug me. But she did extend her hand. Then she walked quickly through the doorway into the cab loading zone.

Back at the apartment, before I unpacked I had to make one phone call:

"Sandy? It's me."

"How are you doing?" She asked.

"I'm fine. Yes, everything went well. Mrs. Livingston had a little trouble, but she's OK. Would you believe, Mrs. Huff won a trophy. So what have you been doing all weekend?"

".What do you mean you don't want to talk about it?"

"Oh! The whole week end?"

"I thought you said you only dated him casually?"

"Oh!"

"What did your parents think about that?"

"That's none of your business."

"Sure it's my business. How long have we known each other? What about all those nice things we said?"

"Things change."

"No! No! Some things don't change!"

"Oh, now wait a minute. I didn't mean that.

. . . Don't be silly. You're not wasting my time. We can still see each other. Give yourself some time to think about it. We're still young."

"Goodby?"

"No! No! Don't say that. Look, I'm sorry if I offended you. Just give it some time to think about it. I'll call you next week and we can discuss it."

"Oh, come on."

"Sandy! . . . Sandy?"

END CHAPTER 8

L– R Mr. Stephens, Edna Wager & Author
at Medal Ball in Del Coronado

Chapter 9

BANKRUPTCY

DETERIORATION OF MY RELATIONSHIP WITH Sandy pained emotionally; but worse, it had psychological-functional effects: I had difficulty concentrating in my classes, in completing assignments and even in the performance of my job at the studio. By whatever intra-personal-relationship mechanisms that control our feelings, I had -- from the first time I saw her -- identified with, or unconsciously decided on her as the final destination in my future. Apparently, I had made a unilateral decision: she certainly did not share it. Losing her now only made this desire stronger (don't psychologists tell us that we want most those things we cannot have?)

Calling her became a futile exercise. We could talk. But when it came time to set a date, something always stood in the way. I soon stopped calling. I'm sure she wanted it that way. With finality came resignation, but not relief.

A possible relationship with Joanne Lavorne hovered as a possibility. Now, however, it had too much the context of "sour grapes." Did I really want "second choice?" I fought it well cerebrally but gave in to it at times viscerally: in the practice rooms -- certainly out of the range of the air-vent-register listening devices -- we often embraced and made foolish statements, promises. Formal dating, however, I still managed to resist -- something she could never quite reconcile. "I may have to leave the studio to get you to loosen up, won't I?" She once stated.

Over the next several months the atmosphere at the studio seemed to change. A portentous cloud gathered directly over it -- management especially. Particularly, the behavior of Rodgers and Stephens changed. They had less to say. We saw them less. They interviewed students less. We had far less new students enrolling for long programs. Of special note, during the usual October-Amalgamation season, Gorbani failed to make an appearance.

"It's the new federal and state laws beginning to take effect," Danny noted, taking a bite out of a piece of pizza at the parlor across the street.

"What laws?"

"Federal and state laws restricting certain sales procedures."

"You mean like not being able to sell "Lifetime" Memberships? Is that why so many fitness centers are going out of business?"

"Right! But I don't think it's defined as Lifetime Membership. I believe it forbids contracts over a certain amount, like $10,000, maybe. But it doesn't just apply to fitness centers. It's everybody."

"That would affect most Amalgamation and other long-term programs also, wouldn't it?"

"Absolutely. But here's a real kicker! Now, I understand, a customer has three days after they sign any kind of a large sales agreement to cancel it. All they have to say is they changed their mind."

"Wow!"

"Yeah, if **we** think wow, what do you think management thinks?"

"I don't think they want to think about it."

"Here's something else. Have you noticed the small metal boxes with the pictures on one side are missing from the tables in the sales-conference rooms?"

"Oh, my God, Yes."

"Times are changing, my friend." Uncharacteristic for Danny, he looked very pensive. He continued as someone I didn't recognize, "I believe the country is changing the way marketing is permitted. Mostly I wonder how that will change how we make a living."

Portentously dark clouds formed and grouped directly over the studio at the 1 PM business meeting. Wednesday, prior to the four-day Thanksgiving break, Rodgers announced that the usual teachers' Christmas bonus would be eliminated this year. Stephens appeared just long enough to state his regrets for the policy change, but that "unmanageable weakening business conditions have forced this." In addition, he noted that the usual inflation-adjusted teachers' pay raise usually going into effect on January 1 would be postponed indefinitely this year.

On a positive note, Rodgers hoped some relief might be on the way: he alluded to the closing of many small, independent dance studios. "Perhaps we will start seeing some of these students enrolling here."

The mood of management and teachers filtered down to the students. "I feel a sense of gloom at the studio I never felt before," Mrs. Wager said. "It's as if it no longer is a fun place to come to the Studio."

"I understand how you feel," I said. "I have the same feeling. It's like we all lost our sense of humor at the same time."

Never having a good understanding of the mechanics of business, I found it difficult to understand the actions of management. Now, however, with the advantage of hindsight, I imagine the problems they encountered had come in stages with varying degrees of severity. And their responses, also, were made in stages.

Stage two came three months later. Rodgers spoke to the teachers at the Friday meeting before the Presidents' Day weekend. "I am going to have to ask for your understanding." He paused just long enough to assess our reactions. "Our options have narrowed to this: we are going to have to ask you all to wait just one week -- until next Friday -- to receive this weeks' pay check." Now he hesitated much longer, increasingly scanning the faces of the teachers. "I understand you all have monetary needs and bills to pay. However, this action is inescapably necessary for us to continue to operate. This payment delay will have a huge cumulative effect on our cash flow. So I ask your understanding."

I don't think anybody truly understood; but what were our options? Certainly, some sought alternative employment; all considered it. This actually helped to alleviate the situation somewhat. When Leferts, a newly hired teacher just six months prior, left the studio, management made no attempt to replace her. It helped to reduce the stressed payroll. In this same mode, management laid off Mr. Phillips, who had only one year of experience. I wondered if I -- never one of management's favorites -- would now get the ax (but then I still had Mrs. Wager who would threaten to quit the studio if they did -- I liked to believe).

The third stage came about in a much less clearly defined and decisive mode: it started with the bank not honoring one or two of the teachers' paychecks. Those teachers, however, would return several days later and receive payment. This situation regressed with time -- over a three or four week period -- to where only those cashing their checks early received payment. It reverted to an almost humorous, literal race to the bank on Friday to see who would get paid. This only lasted two weeks.

Stage four, the final stage, took place the following Monday when the studio doors did not open. At 1 PM students and teachers stood outside on the sidewalk talking to Rodgers. Carol Dixon had slips to hand out to all the teachers who needed them to make claims (to the bankruptcy courts) for back pay. She also had the forms to fill out to apply for unemployment -- a continuing sweetheart.

I don't recall who looked more dejected -- the teachers or the students. I had no students in at that time of the day. Danny and I went over to the pizza parlor across the street and had a cup of coffee. He did not know what he would do. He might move back to Los Angeles. Ruben Rodrigues thought he would try to get a job at the San Francisco Studio (not that they would be on a hiring binge themselves). I couldn't commute that far.

I sent a note to my students explaining what I understood of the situation. I wished them well, hoping that I would see them again somehow. I visited Edna Wager at her home and had dinner with her on several occasions. I suggested that she have the San Francisco Studio honor her lessons. "I can't travel that far two or three times a week," she said. "It's just too far. I'm not twenty-five years old anymore."

Speaking of dejected, I, myself, did not exactly feel ebullient: I had lost Sandy; was doing less than poorly in my schooling – due, in part, to the emotional stress with Sandy and my failing job (I had to drop two subjects in the fall term to avoid failing grades). And now, in fact, I had lost my job. In summation, I had lost my girl, my job, and effectively failed in my educational effort. Most pressing, I did not have the cash to make my room payment in three weeks.

Easter (spring break) I spent applying for a "starter" type job in the canning industry (a major employer in the San Jose area in the sixties). Perhaps I could work my way up in an industrial setting. I would give up my ambition to become an engineer. Perhaps the partial education I had acquired at school would allow me to advance more rapidly.

"So what experience do you have in the canning business?" The shop foreman had a cut over his bushy black eyelids that seemed to focus all your attention. "Who did you work for before you applied here?"

"Arthur Murray," I answered.

"Who!?"

"Arthur Murray," I replied. "I taught dancing."

"Oh?" He said, looking up at me suspiciously under his thick eyelids.

"Well, I managed people to an extent. You know, experience handling people. I had students I directed -- in a class, at a veteran's hospital in Palo Alto."

"Oh?"

Mr. Santillo didn't say anything for several seconds. He walked over and looked out the window of the small foreman's shed. Finally, he looked at me slowly up and down. When he spoke the words came out dry and listless. "Just fill out this form. We will have to get back to you later." I am still waiting for his response.

During the summer vacation at school, I began employment-hunting in earnest. To my advantage I had more hours in the day than most people: I did not have to waste the time required to eat three meals a day: I managed to get by on one meal a day at a local buffet where you could eat all you wanted. I ate more than three other people would want. I often wondered how much money they lost each time I ate there. Unfortunately, even this could not go on indefinitely.

After the third month of my unemployment, I walked slowly down the sidewalks of Santa Clara Street, "main street," San Jose. As I walked I thought I heard the familiar sounds of Tango music. Looking about I could not see where it came from. When I stepped back into the street, however, I could see its origin. On the second floor, above a laundry business, the top half of an open window had a blaring yellow sign reading Fred Astaire Dance Studio (NOW OPEN).

Racing up the stairs two flights at a time I fell at the top landing. A tall, handsome, far-eastern-appearing man in his early thirties with thick black hair and a Grecian nose grasped my hand and offered to help me up.

"Thanks, I'm OK," I responded. When I made it to my feet I asked him, "Do you work here."

He spoke perfect English -- with some idiosyncrasies. "Well, I guess I do. I unn this studio."

"Oh," I answered. "Well, I was intending to apply for a job as a teacher."

He had a wide, white-toothed smile. "Well, I hup your dancing is smuther than your stair climbing."

I smiled. "I'm working on it," I said, grasping the handrail with one hand and his hand with the other. "Are you just opening?"

"Yes, next Monday. Hi," he continued. "My name is Marvin Armani." He turned and opened a door to a single room about half the size of our main ballroom. The windows exited out onto Santa Clara Street. Opposite, mirrors extended the full length of the wall except for three small door entries into small conference rooms. Wall speakers blared the completion of an Argentine Tango. "This is our landscape," he said.

"You do it all here, in this one room?"

"Of course!" His thick, black eyebrows narrowed. "Why not?"

"Where will you teach private lessons?"

"Here!" He said. "We merely section off a portion of floor space with curtains to obtain a little privacy." He pointed with his finger. "See the rails in the ceiling?"

He then placed his hands on his hips. He looked directly at me. "So! You want to teach dancing? Have you worked before? If so, where?"

"I worked for Arthur Murray for three and a half years at the Palo Alto and San Jose Studios," I answered.

"Oh! Over there on Alameda Boulevard?"

"Yes."

"I read about them going bankrupt in the Mercury News. They must have operated a lot different than we intend to operate." He thought for a moment. "We don't have their facilities here. We hope to attract more beginner students."

"Can you put me to work?"

"Come back here un Monday. We'll work out something."

Still on summer vacation, I came to the studio early on the following Monday. By noon the single room boomed with the sound of a West Coast swing. It projected out into the street below. On the entrance a large banner read "Opening Day, visitors welcome." Up the stairs, looking in the doorway, several figures turned, lunged and snapped their legs by the large wall to floor mirrors. Mr. Armani met me at the door. He introduced me to the people in the room, including a tall, also middle-eastern, lady with a very slender face and dark, deep-set eyes. "We only have a staff of four teachers," he noted. "Miss Rajec and I will handle all the "junioring" of new students." I then followed him into one of the small rooms he used as an office and filled out the employment application.

Mr. Armani had initiated an extensive advertising campaign on KGO radio and the Mercury News, the local media. After 1 PM the doorway to the ballroom swung open regularly. Mr. Armani or Miss Rajec worked continuously till 10 PM. I practiced some of the different steps from what I had had at Arthur Murray. At 10:30 Mr. Armani and Miss Rajec met me leaving at the stairway. "Good start, wasn't it?" he said. "We're going out for a bite to eat. We dit not half a chance all day."

Because Mr. Armani and Miss Rajec did all the junioring, the teachers did not get students assigned to them for most of the first month. Fortunately for me, Mr. Armani advanced the teachers paychecks to sustain them till they could pay it back with teaching hours. And, we received some pay for attending regular administrative and training sessions. I could thereby make my monthly room payment and improve my diet.

The students I started receiving from Mr. Armani differed from those I had become accustomed to: generally younger, less dancing experience and with less long-term dancing goals (I might add "less articulate," perhaps, but that would sound pedantic or judgmental). One quality, however, they all had without question and without variance: all felt noxiously unhappy about having to change from Mr. Armani to a new teacher (one young lady threatened to sue the studio for past as well as her future lesson-plan finances). "I'm afraid I spoil these women." he would say. Whatever he did, they all came with an irrevocable distain for me as if I had physically ripped them out of the arms or their beloved teacher. I often wondered what this "spoiling" process actually consisted of.

I found these students difficult to teach. And, it stressed me as much. They seemed to retain a long-lasting unfriendly bias towards me I could never quite correct – even with time. Also, I had become spoiled having worked so long at the spacious Alameda Studio -- difficulty adjusting to the limited facilities at the one-main-room studio. The curtains did not provide the privacy to concentrate adequately. One of my students walked off a lesson when I slammed the curtain shut one afternoon. I thought I would get fired.

More seriously, after the initial influx of students following the initial advertising campaign, enrollment dropped precipitously.

183

Fortunately for me, I had more experience than most of the other teachers. I survived "staff reductions." I had very low teaching hours, however, and barely made my room payments.

When sales deteriorated, however, Armani would mount another advertising campaign. (He must have had hidden wealth somewhere. To come up with significant cash outlays never appeared a problem for him.) This would spike enrollment for a short period. However, after many repetitions, the fluctuating-enrollment curve had a downward rather than an upward bias to its slope. This troubled me. Of course, it troubled Mr. Armani more.

Miss Richards, an approaching-middle-age student, had genuine, root-red hair and a Peter Pan upturned-nose. Presented to me on my third month at the studio, from our first introduction, she acted friendly towards me. She had none of the usual separation problems from her juniorer, Mr. Armani. Most importantly, she had serious dance goals and came in three times a week for several hours. She became the "Mrs. Wager" for me of the Fred Astaire Studio.

The loss of my job at Arthur Murray, my unemployment time, and finally my much fewer teaching hours at Fred Astaire had one serendipitous benefit: it allowed more time to study. This could not have come at a more crucial time. My grade point average, as it now stood, did not approach what I needed to graduate. Having been advised repeatedly to down grade to a lesser field of study and not having done so, I faced the possibility of immediate expulsion from school.

At the beginning of the summer vacation, while looking for work, I started something I had never done before: I purchased the books for my next semester's classes. With so much time on my hands, I read them to completion over the summer vacation. This had two benefits. Not only did I better understand the material presented in class, but I had a multi-stroke-handicap-lead over the other students in the classes. In addition, with so few teaching hours at the Fred Astaire Studio, I had far more time to devote to study during the school year. With these new conditions, I hoped for a chance to salvage my educational career. I would certainly have to wait and see.

Yes, I saw Joann Lavorne after the Alameda Studio Bankruptcy -- on formal dates, in fact (no longer restricted by the Arthur Murray student/teacher policy taboo). However, our relationship lacked the feverish excitement it had previously -- from both sides of the relationship: I no longer held the "teacher/student" power-status-advantage over her (as Henry Kissinger once noted, "power is a great aphrodisiac"); and, I could not -- especially now -- fully erase Sandy from my mind when we dated. Looking at Joanne, I would often see Sandy's face. Our dates, therefore, became less rather than more frequent with time.

As the winter season (if you really want to call it winter in California) progressed into its later stages, dark clouds now gathered in intensity at the Fred Astaire Studio. I had gained a closely-guarded respect for Mr. Armani. He truly attempted in a sincere manner to make the business successful -- to endure. I assessed his motives as an honest effort to protect the students' commitments and his employee's jobs. Also to his students who had made irrevocable financial commitments. He often shared these personal feelings with me. However, something evidently did not match the template for a successful business enterprise (like the store front that you see change hands over and over with new ownership never seeming to last more than a short year or two). The problem may have been the lack of space to teach lessons in a private and comfortable manner. Whatever the exigencies lacking, it became evident to all (especially the gossip circle) that the status quo could not continue long. By three weeks before Christmas we had reduced the teacher staff (less the two juniorers) to only three.

Now my status became tentative again at best: "No! You are not going to come to work to find the doors locked," Mr. Armani noted. "I'll let you know before that happens. But you are right. I don't know how long we can stay open with conditions as they are." He looked out onto the truck unloading garbage areas in the space between the buildings in the rear of Santa Clara Street. "You know, my family always wanted me to be a lawyer. They offered to send me to school at Harvard. How do you say it? They half the money. In my country lawyers are synonymous with Gods." He walked over and shut the door to the small ballroom. "I just wunted to dance. When I got to be a good dancer, I just wunted to unn my unn studio. Why? It's as if nothing else had value to me. Why do ve wunt these things?"

"I don't know." I replied. "But I know exactly what you mean." Now I looked out the window. "All I want is a home with a wife that meets me at the door and sits down to dinner with me at the same table every night; and, have a simple, steady, 9 to 5 job. That's not very exciting, is it? But that's all I want."

"Why don't you do it?"

"Well, mostly, I can't convince that one person to sit down with me for the dinners."

"Oh, yes, I know how that can be. But you are a nice man. I am surprised."

"Well, I have other problems, also."

"I see." Now Mr. Armani stopped talking and looked directly at me for a long time without saying a word. When he spoke the words came out monotone as if he were talking into a pipe, without inflection or color:

"Between you and I. I tell you this so you can prepare. . . . I can't keep pooring money dun the sink. . . .The end of this month -- unless

186

something very extraordinary happin -- three weeks. . . . How do you say it? That's all she rut."

"Thank you," I said. "I appreciate knowing that."

My appreciation for knowing Mr. Armani's intentions did little to solace me. Again I faced unmanageable unemployment. My paycheck for the next three weeks would allow me to make only one more room payment. Moreover, I would not have adequate funds to pay my tuition for the spring semester. Now my discouragement even affected my ability to concentrate on my studies, a condition I had not regressed too previously. Any effort now seemed unconditionally futile. If I had reached a low point in status about four months previous, I had just formed a new even lower nadir on the curve.

With few but scattered teaching hours, I spent much time in one of the small rooms at the studio or in the main ballroom idle, sitting, or frivolously practicing a dance movement -- wasting time till I had a lesson (too much time to just sit, but not enough time to start anything constructive.) About a week after Mr. Armani's confiding his intentions to me, I sat on a fold-up chair in a curtained area in the main ballroom. My two arms on my knees supported my head. My eyes glared at the floor. My eyes finally closed and I dozed off to sleep.

Someone must have come into the ballroom and slipped behind the curtain. I felt the warmth and weight of a hand on the top of my shoulder. I woke with a start to see a rather short, black-haired man with a Charlie Chaplin-like stance directly in front of me. His variegated dress exhibited a flaming bright-red tie, a pale-green shirt and a blue suit. He had a wide constantly-fixed smile across his square face that continued as he spoke:

"Mr. Warner?"

"Yes."

He extended his hand as I stood up. He spoke with an English accent. "Hi. I'm John McKnight. Mrs. Dixon informed me that you were here." He now stood facing me and placed one fist into the palm of his other hand. One of the teachers walked by looking at us, but paid no attention. "I just bought the Arthur Murray Studio on The Alameda last week." He paused an instant looking me up and down. "I understand you worked there for several years."

"That's right."

"How would you like to come back and work for me?"

I wanted to wrap my arms around this penguin-caricature-looking man, hug him and scream in his ear, *"You bet your $500 dollar pin-striped suit I would,"* but I controlled myself, and I said that I would come over to the studio tomorrow and we could talk about terms of possible employment (I had not learned much, but I had learned **something** about negotiation over the last four years).

When I had arrived at the steps leading up to the Alameda Studio entrance, it had not changed in its outward appearance in any manner. It felt wonderful just walking up those long steps again. Carol Dixon already sat at the receptionist's desk in the front lobby. A long hug and conversation followed. She looked as if she had lost some weight. "I really missed seeing everybody," she said.

Mr. McKnight cited the same employee pay structure and benefits as had existed with the previous owners. After signing the new employment papers I walked down to the main ballroom. It never failed to charm me: Such a perfect setting with the outdoor atrium on the far end and the stairway landing coming down to the tabled serving and seating area on the other and mirrors on the other two walls. I couldn't help comparing these facilities to those by which Mr. Armani tried to operate.

Mr. Armani had no problem with my leaving. "I am happy for you," he said. "And, you know, with less staff expenses, perhaps,

Miss. Rajec and I -- with only two long-term teachers -- may be able to stay open longer." He looked up at the ceiling. "It might eeffen "fly" thut way."

"I hope it does." I said, as I started to get up to leave. "You certainly deserve it."

"Thank you," he answered, standing to extend his hand. He smiled. "And I hope you have your "dinners" together soom day. Dunt give up!"

"Thank you."

If you said that the teachers felt good about coming back to work you would have to say that the students were ecstatic about resuming their lessons. As per policy, McKnight honored the hours purchased by the students under the previous owners (some significant, but not necessarily complete, reimbursement for these expenses would come out of the bankruptcy proceedings).

To say it felt wonderful to see and greet the students on their return to the studio would understate the experience by numerical factors. Some of the returning students actually had tears in their eyes. Teachers who didn't had strong self control. Mrs. Wager, Jano, Livingston, Huff or Miss Fenner had not changed in any apparent manner. I visited Mrs. Wager at her home that evening to help her decide on the hours she would come in to the studio. Also, the conditions relating to honoring of the lessons had some minor "liability" exclusions I wanted her to understand.

Miss Lavorne did not return. I had not contacted her in over two weeks myself. I puzzled at first. Carol Dixon said that she tried to call her, but her phone number had been canceled. I tried myself and had the same result.

McKnight hired back almost all of the previous staff with the exception of Miss Hudson who moved to San Francisco and now worked at that studio. Even Rodgers came back as executive director. Stephens, rumors said, moved to Los Angeles and managed a car dealership. I don't know what became of Reed.

The new owner seemed to have a good business sense. On the first Friday of the return week, he canceled all lessons at the studio after 6 PM and had an extravagant totally complementary "student welcoming home" party. He catered food and beverages from a wedding promotion company and filled the large ballroom with balloons and other festive decorations. A six-piece Latin band capable of playing all the dance rhythms occupied a corner of the room next to the atrium. He invited not only existing students but everyone who had ever made a contact with the studio in the past.

The ballroom filled much fuller than I had ever seen. After several hours, it became necessary to scream to converse. The dance floor, however, always provided the focus. With the help of all the teachers, the pattern on the floor moved perfectly in the counter-clockwise direction around the periphery of a huge oval for all the "smooth" dances (Foxtrot, Tango, Waltz and Viennese Waltz). For the Latin dances (Rumba, Mambo and Samba), the entire floor filled homogeneously with no hole at its center.

I don't believe any one student left the party before midnight. By 1 AM most either sashayed across the floor with a teacher or another student. Or, they stood against one of the mirrored walls talking loudly with someone. The band stopped playing at 2 AM. Despite the band's exit and the late hour, students seemed reluctant to want to call it an evening. They still talked in groups. Remaining students hugged their farewells with the teachers and walked slowly down the front steps. Rodgers stood at the bottom with a flashlight lighting the steps. By 3 AM the teachers, food caterers and the party-production company had the ballroom cleaned up. The new owners attempt to ingratiate himself with the students had most certainly succeeded.

Mr. McKnight attended all the daily operational meetings at 1 o'clock. He made a sincere effort to have the teachers understand the new marketing ground rules. He had a simple strategic plan: to grow the student body -- to appeal to a whole new population of potential dancers. "If we make the students we have happy, including the newer ones, they will attract others in a self-perpetuating growing circle of new students." The studio owner's Irish-English eyes always appeared to hint of a smile, especially when he spoke. "We can no longer depend on a small fixed number of students to make large one-time commitments. We require many students making lesser commitments. The operating word is 'excitement.' We have to keep our students excited about their dancing." McKnight hesitated for a moment carefully selecting his words. Uncharacteristically, his face lost its hint of a smile for an instant: "If we don't, trust me, we will not be able to prevail -- to continue to operate -- in this new business environment."

With the coming of the spring season in the Santa Clara Valley, McKnight's strategies appeared on target: the advertising campaign he funded in San Jose received support from one funded by the Arthur Murray Corporation nationally. I began seeing many new, and younger, students walking up the front steps. Rodgers had to convert Mr. Rodrigues and Mrs. Watson from long term to junioring teachers to handle the influx of new students.

Teaching the wave of younger students (for me, women) had its benefits and shortcomings: though physically more exciting to dance with, and able to learn certain moves more easily, they lacked the commitment to their dancing the older students had; and, they were more difficult to handle: they often wanted you to teach them in a manner different from accepted and proven professional standard procedures. "I have a boyfriend that dances. I need to learn to do the Tango by this weekend." Or, "I saw a movie last month where they did the Meringue. I just want to learn to do that." They did not adjust well to authority. The Studio and teachers would prefer them much more malleable. They too often merely wanted to "do their own thing."

"The whole dance business is changing," Danny said, as we sat at dinner in the pizza parlor across the street. "In fact, I think that the way America markets products and services is changing. It's becoming a "buyers" world. It's becoming seller beware, rather than buyer beware -- beware of laws that can land you in jail."

Perhaps because Danny had been in the dance business so much longer than I, he seemed to have a keen sense of the business world. "Sometimes I wonder," he continued. "if the people make the times -- or the times make the people."

"What do you mean by that," I asked.

"Well, think about it: do the people in the dance business, the fitness centers, the dating services, and the country clubs all the way down to the automobile dealerships operate in the manner they do because of the existing laws; or, do we have the existing laws because of the way the people operate?"

"Mute point, isn't it?"

"That's right. What is important is for the businesses to adjust. That will determine the survivors."

Now mid-May, the rains in the Santa Clara Valley began to taper off. You define the word "winter" in Bay Area California as "rain." That having ended, the region begins its 6 or 7 month desert climate (from June through November it may rain two days.

With my regular students back at the studio and my obtaining of new students I could easily pay my rent and return to a regular diet. At school, the spring semester had ended. Because I had more available time over the last six months and did the extra summer study, I managed to receive minimally-passing grades for the spring semester.

This, at least, prevented my expulsion from the program. It may have only bought me some time, however. My overall grade-point average still did not approach what I needed to graduate. This summer I would repeat preemptory summer study. Also, I would register for even less units. This recovery-like scenario had one very uncertain, but absolutely necessary condition: that McKnight's strategic plan for keeping the studio profitable -- and in operation -- succeed.

END CHAPTER 9

Dorothy Jano receives her trophy at Medal Ball in Del Coronado

Chapter 10

RAPPROCHEMENT

"Is EVERYBODY HAVING A GOOD time?" Mr. McKight's British accent sounded pleasantly shrill to the mass of dancers standing on the floor below waiting for the orchestra to begin the next selection.

The crowd screamed back an enthusiastic "Yes!"

The studio owner, exhibiting his continuous smile, leaned against the railing. He stood on the landing at the entrance leading down the 5 or 6 steps to the ballroom floor. "You ain't seen nothing yet. Wait until you all do the Copa Cabana with Mr. Rodgers leading the train." The crowd on the floor clapped and whistled. McKnight slammed down the steps two at a time and slid over to where Dorothy Huff sat along the wall. Like a marionette he stood erect, bowed and extended his hand. "I understand they are about to do a Tango, Mrs. Huff. Shall we give it a bloody whirl?" She smiled, stood up, took his hand and curtsied. Standing only a few inches taller than she, he led her onto the floor. They joined the mass of bodies gliding in a counterclockwise loop around the ballroom. What the demonstrative studio owner may have lacked in dancing style and expertise, he made up for with poise, posture and animation. He "showed off" his partners well.

"One thing Mr. McKnight certainly does well is throw a party," Mrs. Wager offered as I sat with her, Mrs. Newbold and Mrs. Jano at a table close to the food pantry. The orchestra had taken a twenty-minute break.

"Yes, he certainly doesn't spare the expenses. We have never had live bands for our weekly parties; and the food caterer is wonderful," Mrs. Newbold exclaimed. "Have you tried the crab truffles?"

"I haven't gotten past the punch bowl yet," Mrs. Jano quipped. "That stuff is not as benign as it tastes."

"I found that out with one glass," Mrs. Wager said.

I glanced around the table at this small group who had been so influential in my dancing career -- and would unquestionably affect how long it continued. Having said very little since we sat down, I finally leaned across the table into the center of the group and in a confidential tone asked, "So! Tell me. How do you all feel?"

"About what?" Mrs. Jano replied.

"The management, the teachers, the studio, your dancing, your treatment, the whole situation here now."

Now the three older women became quiet and looked pensively at each other and myself.

Mrs. Wager spoke first: "You know, most importantly, it's wonderful just to be back. To see you all and to dance and everything associated with it. And, that the studio honored our lessons" Her speech then slowed. "For the first few months, however, I felt as if we had been downgraded. We had in a sense become a liability rather than a resource -- a debit rather than a credit."

Mrs. Newbold joined in: "That's right. The attention was on the new, younger students. We were all just pariahs -- anachronisms from the past. Yes! I was upset." She stopped talking and looked around the room. Her face brightened and her lips curled in a half smile. "But recently I have reevaluated the situation. Everyone has tried to be fair. Like Edna said, they did honor our hours. And in some respects it's better: we have more men at the parties. Before, we never had enough men to dance with." (The mix of new younger students did come in with a male bias). "Now at the parties we often have more men than women."

Dorothy Jano joined in: "You mention the young men. I have had an interesting experience." She reflected for a moment as if not sure she really wanted to proceed. "It's true that we have an excess of men at the parties. And many of them are quite young. I had this young man dance with me last week at the Friday night party. He wouldn't let me sit down. He danced the "magic step" throughout the Foxtrot, the Tango and even the Waltz. That's evidently the only step he knew." She took a drag on her cigarette before putting it out in the ash tray on the table. "He was so nice -- and so cute. I didn't mind that he couldn't dance well." She hesitated again "I must have at least 30 years on him. Do you know that he asked me to go out with him to Maria's Night Club Saturday to practice our dancing? If I weren't married I'd have gone in a fibrillating heartbeat."

The long days of summer passed quickly. By the end of "daylight savings time" in the fall, McKnight had managed to steer the Studio past the most dangerous financial reefs to, at least, a temporary solvency. This did not happen by chance, or easily: He continued the extensive multi-media advertising campaign for new students on radio, local television and newspaper; he had part-time high-school students leave fliers at the libraries, fitness centers and bus stations; he offered free lessons for bringing friends to the studio. New students beginning bronze lesson plans received pocket calculators (the high-tech rage at the time); he offered a grand prize one week vacation in Maui, Hawaii, for the student, teacher, or walk-in customer who brought in the most students for the month of October. And, as the aesthetic incongruity of the decade, I thought, he placed a large billboard sign on the front lawn of the studio. It showed an attractive young model in much less clothing than a formal dancing gown, clinging to a swirling tuxedo-clad partner.

"I want to meet the model who posed for that poster," Danny joked, as we sat at looking out the window of the pizza parlor across the street. I looked quizzically at him. "What I mean is, I'll bet she's hauling in the bucks."

"She's certainly not hauling around much clothing," I remarked. "Do you ever see our ladies dress like that?"

"No. That's for sure." Danny smiled. "And, you never saw Katherine Murray dress like that either -- or ever will."

I laughed, but he continued. "It's all changing."

"What?" I asked.

"The whole dance business. They're targeting an entire different generation." He looked up for a minute. "Actually, it's probably an existential issue. They were forced to do it by the new laws. But now I think they've come to realize they had unwittingly neglected an entire cohort of customers -- the start of the baby boomers: a generation bigger, livelier and more full of the ambition to compete for its share of social success than any other; a cohort shaped and molded by mere numbers into expecting people to notice them; especially in performance-like activities such as dancing."

"Wow! Deep stuff," I remarked, smiling. "Oh, hey, I'm sorry, Danny quipped. "Like I know anything about business. Like I'm a financial consultant rather than a dumb dance teacher. I've been in this racket too long, I guess."

"You do understand business, Danny. You should own your own studio some day."

"Well, actually, I would like to. But that takes something I have never been able to accumulate in great quantities in my lifetime. I'm sure you know what that is."

"Does it start with m and end with y?"

"You are a psychic."

When I arrived home that evening I had a letter in the mailbox. It had no return address. It had no other indication of source other than a San Francisco postal stamping. I threw it automatically in my trash can under my desk *"I get so much advertising junk mail with no return address."* That evening, however, I thought I smelled a haunting scent in my room, as if it lingered, appeared, disappeared and reappeared so faint that I thought I imagined it, yet unquestionably recognizable, familiar and alluring. I searched the room. I inspected the clothes in the closet. I sniffed out the window. My nose finally led me to the trash can. I fetched the letter out and quickly determined it as the source. I did not have to look at the signature at the end. It had come from Joanne. Her depth of thought and sensitivity surprised me: She began by hoping that I would be successful in my studies and find some way to finish school successfully; also, that I would find what I needed in my personal life. She had continued her dancing at the San Francisco Studio and felt so enthusiastic that she hoped to apply for teachers' training on completion of her program. She thanked me for informing her of the training-class opportunities -- and the inspiration.

She went on to confess that she had had very strong emotional feelings about our relationship at one time. She hoped that I did also. "I am sure, however, that you, like I, no longer have those feelings." The letter then went on to mention her fascination with the City of San Francisco, a brief description of her room, her roommate -- a young lady from Australia -- and how she had acquired a pet kitten.

In closing, she noted that she did not require a response to this letter (a mute point since she left no address or phone number). "However," she continued, "The Hyatt Hotel on the North Shore of Lake Tahoe, the view of the ski trails and lake, the hours we spent in the lounge -- and the feelings I had -- will forever remain one of my fondest memories. Best regards, Joanne."

With the November-to-January fall/winter season in Santa
Clara, the short days, long nights and rainy weather gave people
more incentive to do indoor activities (dancing customers at the
studio always ratcheted up during this period.) Likewise, McKnight's
promotions received enough of a response during this time that we
stayed open. In January I received my grades for the fall semester.
Several days later the Men's Dean, Dr Prione, called me to his office
again for a conference. I sat across his massive desk. He spoke slowly
reading a paper on his desk:

"You have managed to register a 2.1 (C-) grade-point average this
semester -- albeit with only 8 units taken. This is almost identical to
your last semester." He looked at me again through the bottom part
of his bifocal lens. "Young man, I appreciate that you are working
full time during your studies. And I understand how that could
affect them. However, as I have mentioned previously, the state of
California cannot make special concessions or have special grading
for each individual circumstance." He looked at a sheet on his desk.
"You have been in the Mechanical Engineering Program for over
6 years. You have taken, counting repeats, well over the amount of
units required for graduation. Unfortunately, because of grades you
cannot graduate."

"I understand that."

"You must also understand that State Schools are tax-subsidized.
We are thereby regulated by the State with certain non-arbitrary
rules -- rules that are not negotiable. We are not allowed to permit
you to take extra classes indiscriminately until you have a proper
grade-point average to graduate."

I closed my eyes and sat erect in my seat. I had spoken with
him enough that I knew exactly what would follow. I could predict
exactly the words the old reprobate would use to tell me that I had
been expelled from school.

Instead of speaking immediately, he stood up from his chair and walked over to the window looking out to the small ad-hoc softball diamond next to the Administration Building. He stood silent, as if trying to decide. He said nothing as I waited. When he returned to his desk, he put his hands on his elbows and leaned toward me. He had a sympathetic expression on his face I had not seen before. His words sounded flat, hesitant:

"Look, trust me, . . . this is beyond my control." (*That's exactly the words I expected*) . . ."But one thing I was able to do. . . You will not believe this, perhaps, but I'll tell you anyhow. I had to put my butt on the line for this. . . .I realize that you have tried hard -- for a long time." He looked at me again. "Maybe it's not much . . .but I was able to get for you one more -- and precisely just one more -- term. . . . Do you understand what I am saying?"

I did not have to hesitate. "Yes I do."

"Are you sure you understand?"

"Absolutely!"

I looked at Dr. Prione in a manner starkly different than I had ever before. I didn't wait for him to excuse me. I stood, shook his hand, turned and walked to the doorway. At the doorway I glanced back at the Dean. He sat with his hands on his desk staring straight ahead. Before closing the door, I stretched my head back into the office.

"Thank you," I said without introduction.

Dr. Prione did not answer. He just shook his head slowly up and down

One term -- approximately four and one half months. And, it would start in three weeks. I sat in my room looking at the wall for that entire Saturday morning.

Monday morning I went directly into McKnight's office. I explained the situation and my proposal as simply but as clearly as I could.

His eyes still had that glint and his smile only faded when he looked at me questionably. "You're saying you would not be taking on any more beginning students. And, you wouldn't be working Wednesdays or evenings?"

"Only Friday evenings -- for the student parties."

"That would cut your working hours about in half, wouldn't it?"

"That's about right."

"I would probably have to hire another teacher to handle the beginning students," McKnight answered, frowning somewhat. But his fixed smile returned. "Fortunately, we have had a pretty good response lately. So I have been considering taking on another male teacher anyhow. Can you make it financially on half your present pay? And, will all this really do you any good at school?"

"To answer your first question, it will pay my rent, food and tuition. I don't know the answer to your second question."

My regular students, Wager, Jano, Fenner, Newbold, Livingston and Huff, normally, came in for their lessons in the afternoon. Those that had hours in the evening, God bless them, readjusted their schedules to the afternoon or Friday evening. I therefore left the studio every day at 5, except on Wednesdays and Fridays.

With the spring weather and the rain abating, McKnight's efforts to attract new students slowed but continued at a satisfactory level. A fall-initiated training class completed in San Francisco and he hired Richard Bloom from the group of finishers. For the next several months, the young man stayed busy enough to sustain himself; the studio stayed busy enough to remain in operation; and I adjusted to my new schedule. The schedule fit my needs and my lifestyle like a pair of Italian leather shoes: Leaving the studio by 5 weekdays, I could prepare my studies for the next day adequately without having to depend on the following morning. Still taking a reduced load, 12 units (four subjects), I had more than adequate time to prepare each day. The reduced pay at work did not allow money for entertainment or social activities -- which I had no time for anyhow. Whether or not these improved study conditions would allow me to get the required much-better-than-average grades I needed to graduate remained a serious question.

Sandy had left no doubt in her position concerning our relationship. No man wants to beg. Consequently I didn't call again. However, who said it? "Hope springs eternal" Perhaps if I showed that I could pass my subjects at school; perhaps if I had more money to take her to nice places; perhaps if I could demonstrate that I could get an adequate job to support a family. Though I did not call, I never gave up thinking it would all work out some day. I could not help thinking how uncertain I had been in my life regarding what I wanted to do with it. But now that I knew, it helped little. What bothered me most was that I had no control over it.

Sandy had grown up in a household that had more than its share of problems: her father, though loving and a good provider, had a large, but manageable, drinking habit. Her mother, influenced by her father, acquired an unmanageable habit. As a result, at the age of twelve, Sandy lost her mother to sclerosis of the liver. Six months after her mother's death, Sandy's father remarried. Sandy, or her brother, could never reconcile this arguably-disrespectful act on her father's part -- particularly the abbreviated timing.

Her grandmother, Mary Agnese Green, having lost her only daughter in an alcohol-related accident, had similar feelings. In particular, she acquired a fervent antipathy for those who drank. Because of the immediate-family problems Sandy had an unusually close and loving relationship with her grandmother. I had had the pleasure of meeting Mrs. Green on three occasions. She worked as a live-in maid and housekeeper for a well-to-do retired company executive in Palo Alto. She also cooked meals and nursed Mrs. Fry (who had a physical problem I never fully understood). We ate dinner and visited with the Fry's and her grandmother twice. On one occasion Sandy and I took Mrs. Green to church.

Sandy must never have told her grandmother my many misgivings. For whatever reason, whether by instinct, the way she talked to me, or just chemically, I always sensed she liked me (Sandy said it was because I didn't drink.).

I now find it difficult to pinpoint the time it happened, but sometime that spring I drifted in my car up Highway 101 and into the city of Palo Alto. I careened about in a random pattern though the old, plush neighborhood streets for at least half an hour indecisively. I recall a patrolman following for two blocks. Seeing him in my rear-view mirror, I turned the corner quickly and pulled over to a stop in front of 245 Middlefield Ave. I exited the car and rang the doorbell.

Mrs. Green seemed surprised to see me. Ada Fry called from the bedroom asking who it was. After informing Mrs. Fry of my identity she invited me to come in. We walked down a long hallway. Mr. Fry sat in the kitchen smoking a pipe. In passing, I waved and asked him how he was doing. He waved his pipe, replied that he was fine, and suggested that I make myself comfortable in the living room.

Sitting down on a couch opposite Mrs. Green, we stared at each other for at least a full minute. She must have assumed that since I had come to her dwelling to see her that I must have something to tell her, or ask her, or show her -- or something, or anything. Unfortunately, the longer I stared at her the less I could think of any purposeful reason for why I had come. Consequently, after several more seconds of embarrassing silence I just asked, "How are you Mrs. Green?"

Sandy's grandmother sat low in her chair. Her short gray hair framed a flat face and short pug nose. Talking, her lips moved but her face showed little expression. When she smiled, however, every part moved, came alive, warmed.

"I'm fine," she answered, still looking at me in a questioning manner.

If the previous period of silence had been clumsy and embarrassing, the following moment surpassed it by whole number factors.

To my surprise, Mrs. Green stood up and walked across the span between the couches and sat down beside me. She placed her hand over mine, smiled and said, "I have not seen you for quite a while. Are you OK?"

"Oh, yes, I'm OK. -- sort of."

"Sort of?"

"No! I'm fine," I answered. "How are you? And how are Mr. and Mrs. Fry?"

"We're not too bad. But Mrs. is not doing too well lately. He's all right."

"Will you stay here forever?" I asked.

"I guess so," she answered. "I don't know what else I would do. When you have no education, you don't have many choices. You said you were going to school, didn't you?"

"Yes."

"How is that going? I think you said once you were having some trouble."

"I think I'm doing better, but it's still a big question."

"Why? You are a smart boy."

"Well, I'm not so sure about that. But, it's a long story. Mostly I didn't allocate enough time to my study. It's my own fault."

"You work too hard."

Mr. Fry came into the room and sat down on the love seat at the other end of the room. Mrs. Green sprung up immediately from her seat beside me, excused herself, and walked quickly into the kitchen. She returned in moments with a cup of tea and a roll on a small tray and handed it to Mr. Fry. She then asked him if he needed anything else. The old man sat in the corner, drank the tea and ate the roll without saying anything to either me or to Mrs. Green.

Mrs. Green and I talked for several more minutes. She placed her hand on my arm. "I have to start to get dinner ready for the Fry's," she said. "Can you stay and have a bite to eat. I'm sure it's O K with Mr."

"Oh! No." I responded. "I couldn't do that. But thank you."

She walked me to the front door. I waved at Mr. And Mrs. Fry now drinking their tea on the same sofa in the living room. At the door Mrs. Green asked me again, "Is there anything I can do for you?"

I hesitated just long enough to make it sound the most foolish: "Talk to her, Mrs. Green. . . . . Please, just talk to her," I said so softly I wasn't sure she heard me.

"You talk to her," she responded, smiling.

"I have, I have -- too much, probably."

Mrs. Green didn't respond to my last remark. She shook her head ever so slightly, smiled politely again, waved again and closed the door.

Driving out onto the freeway, my thought exploded with self immolation and disgust: if in my lifetime I had ever reached a low point in my self esteem, it had came at that moment. I couldn't believe what I had done -- that I could have been such a sniveling wimp: I had crawled on my hands and knees to an eighty-year-old woman and asked her to do my beg-like-bidding for me. If I could do anything to assure that Sandy would never want to see me again, that would surely do it.

The next month passed quickly. We had the week before finals free of classes to prepare for the exams. I tried to figure what I needed to succeed: I had one five-unit class with a laboratory, Thermodynamics (a repeat); four units of Machine Design; and a three unit class in English I had taken because it looked easy. I needed a grade point average better than 3.4, a B+ in the combined 12 units, according to Dr. Prione to bring my overall average above 2.0 -- and eligibility to graduate. I could get an A in the English class, I thought. I still did not "get it" in Thermodynamics -- even repeating the class. The Machine Design class will probably make the difference.

I canceled all my teaching hours the week before the exams. My students understood. I stayed in my one-room apartment all the week, except for the time I spent in the sandwich shop on the corner. By the week's end I felt dizzy. Sunday, I went to the beach at Santa Cruz, 50 miles south of San Jose, and just lay on the sand for half the day.

My first test on Tuesday, in Machine Design, long and tedious, comprised only design problems. I didn't finish the last problem, but felt somewhat comfortable with what I had done. On Wednesday I took the English exam and sailed through it -- I thought. On Friday, I took the Thermodynamics exam: another set of problems I had enormous difficulty with. Only if everyone else had as much difficulty as I did would I have a chance of obtaining even a passing grade, in my estimation.

I lay in my bed on Friday and looked up at the ceiling. I missed not having Sandy to report to at the end of finals-test week -- as I had in the past. I considered what Dr. Prione had told me. I did not have further options after this week. What would I do for employment should I fail to make the necessary grade point average to graduate? I could remain a dance teacher for the rest of my life: lots of excitement, lots of fun, lots or romance; but also, poor pay (in most cases), poor benefits, and ever-diminishing value as you get older {I don't have the business sense to progress into management or studio ownership).

I could try to get a job as a technician at one of the ubiquitous electronics companies nascent throughout the Bay Area. I don't think I would have the patience to handle the minute detail, however. Or, just flip hamburgers at those new places springing up all over with the arches. I might become a manager; maybe even a corporate manager. Yeah, right! I had enough difficulty in trying to mange myself. I had no unquenchable urge to manage other people.

That weekend I returned to Santa Cruz and rented a cheap motel, walked along the beach and ate a late breakfast and dinner at a mom-and-pop restaurant both days. The back booth of the small, one room building faced the beach leading down to the Pacific Ocean. "Mom" cooked on a stove in the same room separated only by a long counter. She had a Slavic, accent, wore a red jacket and talked to all her customers as she cooked. After my fourth visit she started to call me "son." I stayed several hours after eating, drinking coffee and talking to mom. Or, I just looked down the sparsely populated beach to the ocean.

West-coast beaches always disappointed me. As a youngster I recall watching fat old ladies wade out into the shallow, calm, crowded East-Coast surf about a hundred yards, stand and splash water up on their thighs with the tips of their fingers. Sun bathers would turn over every ten minutes because of the heat. Here, isolated few, many wearing windbreakers, huddled behind a sand dune looking out at the crashing waves. A dauntless few bounced up and down on the crests further out. At shoreline, others dug their feet in the swirling sand as the undertow tries to throw them over and drag them under the oncoming wave. My friend at school, meteorology major, explained it to me: "prevailing" westerly winds blow cold air from the ocean onto land on the West Coast; East-Coast land-warmed winds blow lazily from land out to sea. This keeps the East Coast beaches and coastal areas warm until late into the night. The opposite happens on the West coast. I understood that. Perhaps I should have majored in meteorology.

When I returned to school the following Monday, the bulletin board in the student-union room stated that grades would be available at Student Services early Friday morning: you could enter your student ID in a machine and it would spit out your grades on a thin slip of paper.

I taught all my regular hours that week. Mrs. Wager asked each of the three days I had a lesson with her if I had heard yet about my grades. I would have to repeat that I would not know till Friday (God bless her, but age may have caught up with her). Mr. McKnight had scheduled the Spring Dance Party to take place at the end of the month. We were encouraged to make sure all our students attended. All my students said they could make it.

On Friday morning I woke early. I dressed and put on my sports jacket. Taking off my jacket I decided to eat breakfast first. After breakfast, I put the jacket on again and headed for the front door. At the door, however, I stopped, turned, took the jacket off, sat down on the couch and turned on the TV. Three hours later, I put the jacket back on and walked to the school. Now almost noon, I stood outside the Student Services room for several moments with my hand on the doorknob. Someone walked out. I stepped back. I dashed though the open doorway, walked over and stood in line. Moments later I slipped out of line and walked quickly out the door into the hall.

"I could get my grades Monday. It didn't matter. The results would certainly be the same."

In the hallway -- feeling foolish and embarrassed -- I slammed my hand against the wall. I walked back towards the Student Services room. When I arrived at the doorway, however, I turned again. This time I walked much quicker.'

Before I reached the doorway, however, a hand grasped my shoulder from behind. Spinning around I looked up into the bottom of Dr. Prione's bifocals. He stepped back and placed his fist up to his mouth studying me carefully. He had the habit of placing his hand in the waist-high pocket of his green blazer jacket and fumbling with keys.

"Well?" He said.

"Sir?"

He had an uncharacteristic whimsical-like smile on his face that distorted the whole bottom of his long face. When he spoke, the words came out uncharacteristically jovial if not comically:

"Well, what do you think about your grades?"

The keys stopped jiggling, but he continued to look down at me through his bifocals.

I hesitated for an uncomfortable instant.

"Sir, I haven't looked."

He looked down at me raising his eyebrows. "You haven't looked? It's noon, and you haven't looked -- yet?"

"No Sir!"

He continued to stare for several seconds.

I had never seen Dr. Prione smile before. His whole face changed: His cheeks folded into thin wrinkles on the side of his long face; all his teeth had a brown color with one missing in the back of his mouth; but his blue eyes glassed over with a warm shine-like quality. He extended his hand.

"Don't worry," he said. "Go ahead and look!"

I stared into his eyes for several seconds. Finally, I grasped the smiling professor's hand. I wanted to wrap my arms around his thin chest and razor-like shoulders and hug him. In the sixties, however, you didn't do that. Instead, I merely squeezed his hand, grasped his elbow with my other hand and said, "Thank you. Thank you. I will." Clumsily, I dropped his hand, said "Thank you" again, turned and walked back towards the Student Services Office. As I left, Dr. Prione merely stood nodding his head slowly up and down.

Now that I knew that I would graduate, I wanted to get up on a table in the cafeteria and scream it over the loudspeaker. I wanted to stop people on the street and tell them. Bustling with confidence and enthusiasm, I mustered up enough courage to call Sandy, but, as usual, I could not reach her.

I started to send out resumes for potential job interviews. On interviews, many companies did not ask for results of grade-point average at college. Some did. Owens Corning, a Fortune-500 rated company -- located in Santa Clara County, the future site of "Silicon Valley" and the technology explosion -- did not. I received an offer to start employment at O C on September 1st, -- in just two months.

At the studio, my students had mixed feelings about my new career. I took Mrs. Wager out to dinner to tell her in the proper manner. Had it not been for her fiercely-unwavering support in the beginning of my teaching, I would never have made it to this position in my life. I wanted her to know that. Also, I wanted her to know that we would always remain special friends. When I said good night to her at her home, she had a tear in her eye. I did also.

For the next several weeks, McNight stressed the coming spring party at the 1 PM business meetings:

"We live or die by the amount of fun that our students have." He pointed to an 8-1/2 by 11 sheet of paper scotch-taped to the blackboard: "This is a list of all our students. I want to see all of them at the party; the only way that happens is that you make sure you ask them."

As noted previously, when McKnight gave a party he went all out: the Mercury News ran an ad promulgating it as the Santa Clara Valley's premier social event of the year. Set for August 18th, just two weeks before starting employment at Owens Corning, I told Mr. McKnight I would end my teaching at the Studio that Friday.

I did not start my students on any new steps; I tried to review everything we had done in the past. Mr. McKnight, always the methodical one, had a replacement for me already designated and in place. I took some time in my lessons to introduce Mr. Hicks to all my students. A seasoned teacher, he had bought a home in San Jose for what he referred to as "the ridiculously-over-inflated price of $18,000."

The last week at the studio seemed longer than my first. I spent most of the last hours with my students sitting and talking: as if talking about what each of us would do in the future would somehow make us share that experience. Despite knowing rationally that in reality it would in no way ever happen. I wanted to know what Dorothy Jano would do in her new home in Mill Valley and how long she would continue to take lessons. I wanted to know if Mrs. Livingston would sometime move to live with her grandchildren she had spoken about so often. Would Helen Fenner ever get another dog to replace the one that had passed away. Even Mrs. Huff let me know she would move to Los Angeles in a few years and live with her daughter.

As I left the Studio each night the last week I would look back up the long steps at the huge elevated residence-appearing house with its entrance on the middle floor. So many memories: The first day I had walked up those steps; how fortunate I had been to make it to here; how unpredictable. Yet, I felt neither pride, satisfaction, nor accomplishment. A huge hole, one could drive a semi-trailer truck through, still existed in my life. Even time, supposedly the unfailing healer, helped little. I thought of her -- or her unavailable presence -- every moment of every day.

The band McKnight hired for the party had at least six members. Three saxophone players' stands formed a line diagonally across the front corner of the ball room. The drummer and xylophone player filled the rest of the corner. The vocalist, the apparent leader of the group, stood on a small low platform in front. The three-wall-mirrored room echoed with the booming sound of the band tuning up their instruments.

By 7 PM the room filled with guests and teachers. The refreshment pantry stood with its shutter-like doors open. Three ladies in bright-colored dresses filled orders in a professional manner. Ladies in long evening dresses and men in dark suits (if not tuxedos) stood around the periphery of the recently-waxed dance floor. Guests continued to come down the stairway at the far end into the ballroom. McKnight stood up on the vocalist's small stand and welcomed everybody in his usual shrill but witty manner. He ended by keeping a promise to quickly "clip his lip" and let everybody "get on" with what they came for -- to dance. Dorothy Jano had arrived first. She smoked as I sat with her at one of the small tables near the entry to the ballroom. I thanked her for being able to share with her the spirit she exhibited for her dancing -- and for life; and how much it had helped boost my own morale over the years.

At about 7:30, when the band started playing, we danced several dances. At the announcement of a "mixer" dance, I thanked her for the dances. I never saw or talked to Dorothy Jano again in my lifetime. After dancing with one of Mr. Rodrigues' students, I saw

Dorothy Huff standing against the wall. I asked her to dance a quick step. I thanked her for forcing me to grow my dancing to meet her level. We had several dances together before another mixer dance separated us. She gave me a long hug when we separated.

Helen Fenner stood against the mirrors looking down at her feet, her hands clasped in front of her waist. She wore a black satin dress with a white blouse. She reminded me of a Seventh Day Adventist going to church. When I asked her to dance she said nothing, but characteristically smiled sweetly and took my hand. We danced a Fox Trot for what became our last dance together. One of the men students cut in and asked her to dance. She did look cute.

I found Mrs. Livingston talking to one of the girls behind the refreshment counter. As we had several dances together I asked her how long she intended to take lessons at the studio. "As long as I can stand without someone having to hold me up," she said. Old pro, Mr. Gonzales stopped by and asked Mrs. Livingston to dance (a practice always encouraged by management to prevent one teacher from spending too much time with any one student at parties). As we parted, she just extended her hand and thanked me for the dance.

As usual, I found it difficult to find an opportunity to dance with Mary Newbold. I finally cut in on her dancing with Mr. Rodrigues. After several dances, one of the students stopped by and asked her to dance. She gave me a long hug. "Just in case I don't see you again," she said. She didn't.

By 10 o'clock I had danced with all my students, except Edna Wager. Always friendly and personable, she had appeared engaged all night. A little after 10, however, after the orchestra had taken a break, I started to cross the floor seeking someone to dance with. People crowded, talking, waiting for the music to start. Mrs. Wager walked quickly towards me and caught me at about the center of the floor. "Hi," she said. "I want to talk to you."

"I have been looking for you all night," I replied. "You have been so busy."

"Oh. Yes. Isn't it wonderful? And, it's such a great party. But, listen, stay right here. Don't move," she said.

"Of course," I replied. As I spoke the band started playing again. I turned my head and listened for a moment. I extended my hand to Mrs. Wager, "I haven't heard that song for a long time."

Mrs. Wager did not take my extended hand. Instead she said, "Wait a moment." In that moment I felt a hand on my shoulder. A voice I would recognize in the middle of a Chinese New Year celebration said softly, "Perhaps no one has requested that song recently!" Snapping around I saw Sandy's hand extended towards me.

"Is West Coast Swing still your favorite dance?" she said smiling. I could not find a word to answer. I peered foolishly. Finally, I nodded my head slowly and took her hand. Mrs. Wager placed her hand on Sandy's arm, smiled and said, "See you two later."

This time, Sandy's hand did not shake, feel moist or cold (she, also, had come a long way in the last five years.). The vocalist had an Asian accent. And, they sounded somewhat tentative in starting to play. It may not have been the best interpretation of "King of the Road" vocally or instrumentally. To me, however, each note echoed majestically across the four corners the ballroom. Through the corner of my eye, I noted Mrs. Wager asking people she knew to sit down. Soon, several others left the floor. Sandy and I were left with a large vacant enclave in the center of the floor to position our West-Coast-Swing slot.

"*Trailers for sale or rent; rooms to let -- fifty cents. . .*" As Sandy's lithe frame sashayed past me in a side pass, she kept her eyes focused straight ahead. Pulling her towards me in a whip-step, her body slammed directly towards the spot I had just vacated by moving to the side. Her body snapped around at the pivot point and glided smoothly backwards down the slot in the opposite direction with a three-step chasse. *". . .Four hours of pushing broom -- buys six by ten four-bit room. . . ."* Pulling her towards me again she took two long gliding steps, extending the palms of her hand. Her entire body mass (all 106 pounds) slammed into my open palms at the "sugar push" and then slid backwards down the slot into another three-step chasse. *". . . Can't have no pool, no pets – ain't got no cigarettes. . . ."* I led her into a series of 8-count "drags," leaning back as if riding a surf board, her right arm trailing, her feet swerving in a zig-zag pattern forward. *". . . Know every engineer on every train, all of the children and all of their names. . . ."* Her steps trailed the music that imperceptible second, giving her movements that sustained, measured, in-control perception. A natural musical instinct -- something you cannot teach.

The dance floor had now completely cleared. I should have felt nervous, or concerned about dancing with an instructor at a party. But the exploding realization that Sandy had actually come to the party flushed out any misapprehension from my consciousness. I enjoyed every moment. Sandy drifted slowly past me again in a side pass. Her sight fixed inexorably forward. Glancing over, I wondered what force of nature had ripped a hole in my chest and gripped my heart with 19th Century ice thongs since the first time I held her hand over five years ago: that damnable-stubborn cant to her head and shoulders as if forever facing into a bracing headwind -- and loving every moment of it; the viral glint in her steel-blue eyes -- the first to lie on the steps of the city hall; the inimitable rolling gestures of her long arms and fingers making a point in a conversation . . .

The band careened to a spasmodically-bumpy ending with all members not finishing together. Sandy and I stood in "open" position at a cleared space in the center of the ballroom. We stared at each other several seconds. She placed her hand on the side of her cheeks.

Rolling her eyes she looked upward. In a loud whisper she shouted, "You talked to my grandmother!?" She repeated, "Oh, my God -- you asked my grandmother to talk to me?"

I turned my back and shrugged my shoulders, now I looked away and did not speak for several seconds.

When I faced Sandy again, she continued to stare. I hoped that I saw the beginning of a smile. She took a step towards me and placed the top of her head on the side of my chin. I carefully placed my arms around her back. The band played an off-beat Samba. I don't remember what else they played or how long we stood in the center of the ballroom. I do remember Sandy saying ever so softly, "We have to talk!"

"When?"

"We can have dinner tomorrow. I'll cook something good."

END

Meryl White & Author at Jack Tarr Hotel in San Francisco

Epilogue

SANDY AND I DID GET married; to this date, we have had 56 years of dinners together. I worked close to 40 years for Owens Corning in Santa Clara, California. We have two children -- girls.

Dancing? Now **we** take the lessons. Where? Where do you suspect?

References

1. https://en.wikipedia.org/wiki/Arthur_Murray.
2. ...*The Scribner Encyclopedia of American Lives: 1997-1999* By KennethJackson
3. ...Obituary *Variety*, March 11, 1991.
4. ...*Arthur Murray. Tech Topics. Georgia Tech Alumni Association. Summer 1991. Archived from the original on 2007-10-12-11 Retrieved 2007-06*
5. ...http://arthurmurray.com/history

Index of Names

A

Ada Fry 204

Al Stephens 45

Arthur Murray v, ix, x, xi, 2, 4, 5, 6, 13, 16, 17, 18, 21, 28, 29, 30, 32, 36, 41, 42, 45, 48, 49, 52, 67, 75, 92, 97, 114, 116, 118, 124, 130, 138, 145, 153, 154, 180, 182, 184, 185, 188, 221

B

Betty Furnace 26

Betty Walcott 20

Bill David 21, 22, 29, 43

Bill Roper 7

Bob Knight 6, 19, 53, 68, 77

Bob Rodgers 46, 53

Bruce Logrin 29, 32

C

Carol Dixon 5, 134, 178, 188, 189

D

Daniel Sanchez 130, 135, 154, 156

Dave Parrot 32

Don Sparks 20

Dorothy Huff 111, 128, 129, 157, 195

Dorothy Jano 47, 59, 61, 64, 67, 69, 70, 77, 82, 94, 95, 96, 101, 197, 212, 213

Dorothy Kelly 48, 57, 59

Dr. Prione 89, 117, 130, 201, 207, 210, 211

E

Edna Wager 47, 64, 67, 77, 133, 179

Eric Strom 20, 45

F

Fred Astaire 2, 8, 92, 153, 181, 184, 185

G

Gale Lofkin 26

H

Helen Renner 65, 67, 70, 77, 83, 95, 120, 212

Herb Ramires 20

J

Jim Peters 10

Joan Darin 4

About the Author

THE AUTHOR GRADUATED FROM SANTA Clara University with a master's degree in mechanical engineering, has worked for forty years in the engineering field, and was awarded several patents in the glass fiber-forming process.

George, however, has written extensively all his life, including five other books: Mentor (historical narrative), Best of Enemies (historical narrative), Living on Lifesavers (memoir), Knee High to Hell (memoir), and How Changing World Demographics Affects Your Investments & Careers (financial).

Instead of rapaciously focusing only on cement, cold steel, and unchangeable physical laws—the holy grail of engineering—during off hours and vacations, his mind danced with ideas for books: conflicts, crises and resolutions, his own and the experiences of others, real and unreal.

The author retired in 2006, giving him more time to focus on writing exclusively. His personal writing now includes six books and a collection of ten short stories. He concurrently served on the board of directors as secretary and newsletter contributor for two NGO nonprofit organizations: World Runners and Global Partners for Development.

Printed in the United States
By Bookmasters